DIG & DIG DEEP

by

Richard Arnold
Private First Class, retired

in Collaboration with:

Guido N. DiMatteo III
and Frederick Gale, MD

Copyright © 2012 by 2 Flowers Publishing.

All rights reserved. No part of this publication may be reproduced, distributed, or transmitted in any form or by any means, including photocopying, recording, or other electronic or mechanical methods, without the prior written permission of the publisher, except in the case of brief quotations embodied in critical reviews and certain other noncommercial uses permitted by copyright law.

Printed in the United States of America

First Printing, 2012

ISBN 978-0-9885029-0-1

2 Flowers Publishing
PO Box 250
Ontario NY, 14519-0250

Email: 2flowerspublishing@gmail.com
Website: www.2flowerspublishing.com

Seventh Edition

The views and opinions expressed in this work do not necessarily reflect those of the contributing parties in the Credits and References section.

Dig & Dig Deep is a memoir of one soldier's WWII experiences.
This book is dedicated to those brave souls who served in the defense of freedom.

To Beth

From day-one eight years ago in 2004, it was my beloved wife Beth and Beth alone, who insisted that this book – now entitled *Dig & Dig Deep* – be the foremost brainchild of our wedded life. For her support, love, and motivation, I am and will always be grateful.

Table of Contents

Chapter 1: Writing on the Wall 8

Chapter 2: Learning to Dig 11

Chapter 3: *Queen Elizabeth* to Cobblestones 19

Chapter 4: Close Calls 28

Chapter 5: Wiped Out on Our First Day of Combat 32

Chapter 6: Your Feet's Too Big! 40

Chapter 7: Battle with No End in Sight 44

Chapter 8: The Surprise of the Ardennes Forest 53

Chapter 9: Saar River Massacre 57

Chapter 10: From Cut to Fill 62

Chapter 11: Advance of the King Tigers 72

Chapter 12: The Luxury of Luxembourg 83

Chapter 13: Who the Hell Are You? 88

Chapter 14: Back to the Front 90

Chapter 15: Frozen Nearly Unto Death 94

Chapter 16: Paris in the Springtime 100

Chapter 17: The Road to Hell 102

Note to the Reader Before Entering Buchenwald 105

Chapter 18: The Master Sergeant, and The Gates of Buchenwald 107

Chapter 19: The Building of Pure Horror 110

Chapter 20: Nocturnal Visitor 121

Chapter 21: A Guided Tour of Evil 123

Chapter 22: Back to the Repple Depple 135

Chapter 23: From Radio to Switchboard 137

Chapter 24: Mistresses, Rations, and Jazz 142

Chapter 25: Radar and Rockets..144

Chapter 26: Usefully Stupid 147

Chapter 27: Furlough to London and Paris...150

Chapter 28: Furlough to Mt. Blanc 158

Chapter 29: Hitler's Lightbulb..161

Chapter 30: The Trip Home 165

Chapter 31: America after the War...171

Afterword: The Pledge as a Work in Progress...173

A Nephew's Perspective...181

For Dad, Who Just Celebrated His 86th Birthday 183

Dedications 188

Acknowledgments...189

Credits and References 190

Bibliographic References...194

About the Author 195

One incredible day, in October of 2010, a little girl, age 3, stood before me, looked me squarely in the eye and recited:

> "I pledge allegiance to the Flag
>
> of the United States of America,
>
> and to the Republic for which it stands,
>
> one Nation, under God, indivisible,
>
> with Liberty and Justice for all."

It was the occasion of my 85th birthday, and it had taken 15 seconds for my great-granddaughter to recite The Pledge of Allegiance from rote. The tears welled up in my eyes — she had just summed up my life, its realities, and its WWII-generated dreams.

Chapter 1: Writing on the Wall

On September 1, 1939, my Dad and I were fishing in the St. Lawrence. It's a big river, and the currents can be tricky — so we were there with our favorite professional guide, Nacky, in his sturdy but simple fishing boat. We were all listening to Dad's "high-tech" radio, a heavy Zenith the size of a breadbox with a long antenna. It was beautiful out, and I was as care-free as an adolescent can be at 13...

Suddenly, Dad's radio gave us the news that Hitler had invaded Poland — World War II had begun!

Before that day, all of my aunts, uncles, and cousins on both sides of my family were writing to us regularly from their small villages in Poland. My parents, who were fluent in Yiddish, would read their letters to me. But in a matter of days, unprepared Poland ceased to exist, and we never heard from any of these relatives again. We know of none who survived in The Old Country from that day forward.

Because of their treaty commitments with Poland, both England and France had to declare war on Germany. By the time I was 15, my father saw the handwriting on the wall: the USA was going to get dragged in - just as in World War I. To protect me, he sent me to The Manlius Military Academy, which had an excellent reputation and was nearby to my hometown of Syracuse, New York. As an ROTC[1] school, it could graduate me as an officer, and therefore, in time of war, I would be more prized for my leadership skills than for dangerous frontline grunt work.

Manlius no longer exists as a military academy. After the war, when all kinds of prep schools went coed, all-male military schools just couldn't make it ("Girls in the military? Get real!").

A couple of months after I turned 16, I hitch-hiked the 12 miles home for an unexpected weekend leave. I let myself in, and as I was walking through the door, the phone rang. I picked up the receiver to hear a friend of my Dad's:

"Son, I'm calling to speak to your Dad. Is he home?"

---

[1] ROTC stands for Reserve Officer Training Corps.

I shouted upstairs, "Hello! Anybody home?" Silence. "No. I'm all alone."

"Do you know the news?"

"What news?"

"Turn on the radio."

I did, and the news was of our huge naval base, Pearl Harbor, being attacked by Japanese planes. I had hitchhiked home on December 7, 1941 — "a date," as President Roosevelt said in his speech to Congress, "which will live in infamy."

At the time of that call, few details were available. In those pre-Internet days, transoceanic communication was very limited. Our sky-scanning radar network was so erratic that when our lookouts reported Japanese planes zeroing-in on Hawaii, our own radar operators were not believed[2].

I was shocked at the audacity of Hitler's buddies in daring to attack our men in Hawaii, but at age 16, I was teenager-sure that the "bad guys" had bitten off more than they could chew. Without any further thought than the horrible stereotyping I had seen in our nation's editorial cartoons, I assumed that the small-sized attackers would have been beaten into the ground by my military school's far more formidably-sized graduates — long before I could be old enough to serve.

The Great Depression was finally ending, but our family's thriving business found us in good financial condition. My father was a guy who pulled strings, so he set about getting very friendly with the major in charge of recruitment in Syracuse, and asked him what I should do to survive the war by staying out of harm's way.

"Well," the major said, "instead of waiting until he reaches 18 and gets drafted, why don't you have him enlist at 17, so he can apply for the ASTP?" He then explained about the Army Specialized Training Program, which took kids with high marks and high IQ's, and instead of putting them on the front lines, sent them to college to learn military government.

---

[2] Hawaii didn't become a State until 1959, but never mind that: our men were being attacked!

"We're planning ahead to the time when people whose towns we liberate will interact with ASTP-trained military until their towns can govern themselves. ASTP men will be safe.

"He'll need to score high on a qualifying exam, but his great report cards from a top-rated military prep school show him to be a first-rate student."

Billy Goldstein, my best friend from our temple's Sunday School, lived on the same street as my family, just a block away on Allen Street. Because we were so close, we had influenced each other in our mutual ambition for engineering degrees at top-rated MIT. Both 17, we took the qualifying test on the same day in Nottingham High School's gym. Billy checked the box for "Navy", but since Manlius was an Army prep school, I checked the "Army" box — about a quarter of an inch away from it, on the same form. We both aced the exam.

While completing our first semester at MIT, we both turned 18. As required, we reported for active duty. Billy went off to the Navy's version of the ASTP, and I went into the Army at Ft. Benning, Georgia. Because I had been sworn in a few months before turning 18, I was listed as having volunteered. I volunteered, but with a "guarantee" that I was at no risk of getting hurt.

I was in favor of that. I had no burning desire to get shot at.

Chapter 2: Learning to Dig

The day before I was to report for active duty at Fort Dix, NJ in November of 1943, I took the train from Syracuse to New York City. I stayed overnight in nearby NJ, at the home of a friend, Ronnie Rinzler. He and his mother had stood just ahead of my Mom and me in the enrollment line on our first day at Manlius two years prior. Now, in honor of my last night as a civilian, he had arranged a date for me with Lynn Fortgang, a gorgeous neighbor of his, whom he had introduced me to at our Junior Prom.

My favorite band, Benny Goodman, was playing at the Hotel New Yorker. Taking a chance, we grabbed the train to the lower end of Manhattan, hoping that there would still be tickets. The concierge advised us that Benny Goodman's "Music in Wartime" show was being filmed tonight, and had therefore long been sold out. When I explained about reporting for active duty the next day, he asked to see my papers. Satisfied, he reached over and picked up a little round table, held it up high over his head, wended his way through the crowd, and finally set the table down right next to the curve of the piano on the stage. The show was fabulous! Benny was in his prime.

Image 1: Benny Goodman and his Orchestra at the New Yorker Hotel 1943

The next day I was on a military bus to Fort Dix, NJ for a two-week induction process, followed by a train ride to Fort Benning, Georgia for 13 weeks of basic training. At the end of the 12th week, the bulletin board finally showed where each of us was going to be sent to college under the ASTP program. I had been assigned to go to Vanderbilt, all expenses paid.

But the very next day, the list was gone!

My drill sergeant announced that the ASTP program was closed, because the Army didn't need *college* students. They needed men who could *fight*, not study.

I remember the lieutenant's speech: "Nobody will apply for either the Air Corps, the Navy, or any other sissy organization. Any such applications will be turned down automatically. You're infantry!" I think they took pleasure in making college guys into lowly, foot-soldier cannon fodder. In those days, high school was as far as most kids ever hoped to reach.

After basic, I was sent to Fort Jackson, South Carolina, where I joined the 87th Golden Acorn Division.

Image 2: 87th Division Shoulder Sleeve Insignia

It was an old unit that had been deactivated after The Great War (the earlier name for World War I), and had been serving as a Tennessee hill-country National Guard unit. Reactivation meant that it reverted to Regular Army. They scattered our small number of high-score teenagers throughout the Division. In the Company I wound up in, Company A of the 346th Regiment of the 87th Division, I knew only one other guy. The other kids resented us because we were different. In those days, in Tennessee, high school graduates were rare. For my part, I could hardly understand some of their backwoods accents, so I was certainly not accepted by them.

For some unknown reason, with American soldiers fighting a global war, and manpower in short supply, we went nowhere. Lacking other instructions, our commanders simply opted for doing Basic Training over, and over, and over. I had already *had* basic training up the yin-yang at military school, and at Fort Benning. Now, they had us digging and refilling practice foxholes[3] until our *blisters* had blisters! The old WWI Manual that served as our textbook told us to dig holes as deep as we were tall; but one of our instructors — (who had actually served on the front line) — told us that was all wrong. He said:

"The first thing you do is dig a *shallow* rectangular hole: make it as long as you are tall, as wide as your body is wide, and as deep as your body is thick. That way, when you're under fire, you can dive full length and fall face down into it for protection at the earliest possible moment. Later, when the firing eases up, you can make the foxhole deep enough to stand up in for maximum protection."

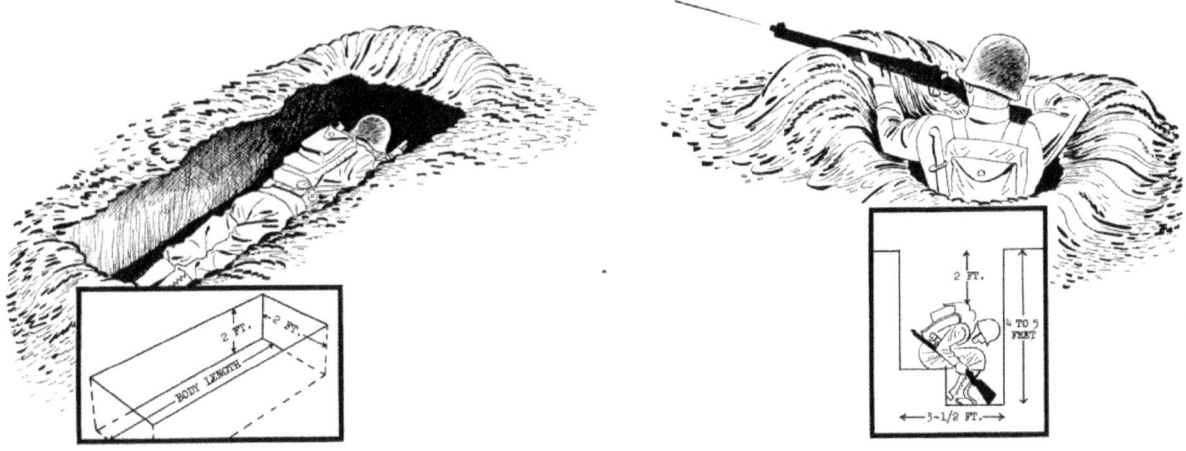

Image 3: Prone Foxhole   **Image 4: Standing Foxhole**

At one point, when I was doing *anything* to get out of that endless, stupid basic training, I broke a fundamental infantry rule: "Never volunteer for anything!" When they asked for volunteers to go to radio school, I raised my hand. I didn't know it yet, but this was incredibly stupid for a guy whose main goal was to survive the war.

---

[3] Foxhole: a small pit, usually for one or two soldiers, dug as a shelter in a battle area.
http://dictionary.reference.com/browse/foxhole.

Radio training took me to a base in North Carolina for several weeks, where the school was just a barracks cleared of its beds. There were folding chairs set up around tables loaded with radios, headsets, and spare batteries. (No such thing as rechargeable batteries in those days.)

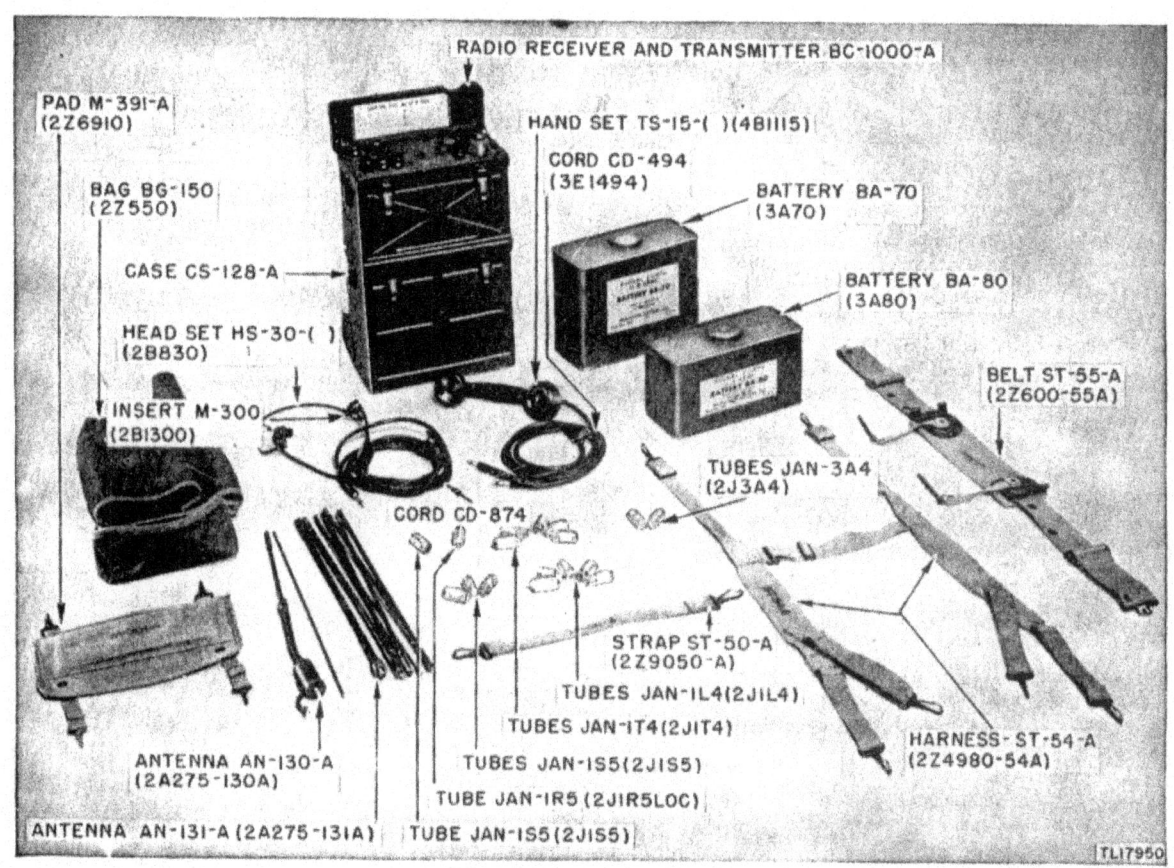

Image 5: SCR-300-A Radio Set

I spent weeks learning not only Morse code, but also the radio protocol that had to be memorized, how to operate and field-repair the equipment, and tricks for memorizing codebooks. It was drilled into us how quickly we had to memorize our codebooks. Also critical: we had to be concise and get off the air as soon as possible, so as to avoid being located by the enemy triangulation teams always monitoring our radio communications traffic. Though the time spent in radio school was a great temporary diversion from the repetitive basic training, it turned out that I was carelessly setting myself up for a position that was among the most dangerous. My father, who had pulled all the strings to get me into the immediately defunct

Army ASTP as a way to keep me safe, had unwittingly combined with my own stupidity to set me up as a frontline combat radio operator.

After the brief respite of radio school, I found myself back in the endless basic training cycles at Fort Jackson, and I couldn't take it anymore. That South Carolina sand was hot! So, I went to the Special Services officer with a proposal:

"How about having a battalion newspaper?"

"Yeah, that's a good idea."

I told him my credentials: I had taken a printing course in high school. I did the editing, personally set the type, and ran the printing press for my military school newspaper.

"Alright, Private Arnold, go for it. But you don't get outta Basic training."

"But, I've already been, and been, and been there."

"Never mind. You wanna do a newspaper…do it on weekends with my blessing. But *no one* gets outta Basic!"

I made the same weekend deal with the closest local printer. He was happy to let me work his equipment on Sunday. It was good business for him: paper was strictly rationed because of the war, but I could bring him Army paper, which meant that he would have nothing but clear profit to show for my producing a morale-building Army newsletter.

The Special Services gave me an office in their barracks, which housed the marching band and other miscellaneous personnel. I remember listening to the marching band practice as I worked. I would line up Coca Colas on the windowsill and, filled with caffeine, stay up most of the night writing and editing the newspaper. Then at 5:00 in the morning, I'd be back with my platoon to continue the compulsory basic training all day[4]. The printer gave me a key to his shop, where I did the typesetting and printing. When I published the first issue, I included a front page column complete with photograph entitled, "The Colonel Speaks".

---

[4] To avoid confusion, military time doesn't use a 12-hour clock. It uses a 24-hour clock. Five in the morning would be written as 0500, and spoken as "zero five hundred hours", "zero five hundred", or "Oh five hundred hours", or "Oh five hundred". Five in the evening is written as 1700, and spoken as "seventeen hundred hours", or "seventeen hundred".

I had just started on the second issue when I passed out cold, due to lack of sleep. They sent me to the hospital and the doctor said it was fatigue. When the colonel found out that without me, we weren't gonna have a newspaper anymore, and his column "The Colonel Speaks" wouldn't be on anymore front pages, he said, "From now on, Private Arnold is Editor of the newspaper and does not take any more basic training."

My strategy had worked — no more practice foxhole digging for me!

I redoubled my editing and printing efforts. Among the Golden Acorn men in my division, the paper's most popular feature was the comic strip character I created, named "Acorn E. Yending". Said quickly, he was "A Corny Ending". The name I gave the newspaper was *The Countersign*. (In an encampment, when someone approached a sentry box, the man on duty would ask for that hour's security sign; and you would need to respond with the appropriate countersign. An example would be the sign "Henry" and the countersign "Ford". That way you were both assured that neither was an imposter.)

Happy as I was for this respite, there was always a question in the back of our minds: Why is our already basic-trained infantry division sitting here idle in the States while there's a global war going on? I didn't know why, but we were lucky: the high casualty landings in Normandy were taking place, a lot was happening in the South Pacific, and meanwhile, we were a full strength division[5] not getting shot at…and though some of us were itching to fight, I personally had no complaints about being safe in the good old USA.

Up until that point, we had a first lieutenant in charge of our partial company (full companies are led by captains). Our Lieutenant was a good man, and knowing that my sister Lois's wedding was coming up, I made a deal with him: I would forgo all time off for three months, in exchange for being allowed to go home the one weekend of her wedding.

A while before we were to leave for war, we got our new captain — who told me I could forget about the wedding. *He* had made no promises to me, and would not honor one made by someone else.

I thought, Whoa, this isn't just *any* weekend we're talking about! Lois is one of my sisters, and she always looked out for me when I was a kid. Lois was four years older than I,

---

[5] In a US infantry division numbering 15,000 men in WWII, about 3,000 were frontline fighting men; the rest were vital support troops, including truck drivers, materiel management, cooks, etc.

and when she came home from camp, she would teach me the new songs she had learned. We, and our sister Dorothy, were natural harmonizers. Then there was this important memory: friends and family always called me Dickie when I was little. One day, Lois said to me, "You know, you're getting to be quite a young man. Maybe it's time for people to forget about calling you Dickie. Let 'em learn to speak to you like the man you're becoming." Made sense, and I let people know. After that, everyone let go of the diminutive "ie", and started addressing me as Richard or Dick.

So, after trading a whole quarter-of-a-year's worth of leave time in order to see my beloved red-headed sister wed, my new commanding officer had given me no option as a devoted brother but to go AWOL[6].

After formation ended at 1700 hours on the appointed Friday evening, I calmly walked out of the gates of Fort Jackson, SC. I knew that with the country at war, and me wearing a soldier's uniform, hitch-hiking would be easy. In no time, a truck picked me up, and took me to the coast. From Jacksonville, Florida, I caught the Atlantic Seaboard train to Penn Station in New York City, and made my way to Grand Central. In those days, the open areas of the train station had cots for traveling soldiers to nap on, and I flopped there for a few hours before catching the early Empire State Express. I made it home to Syracuse in time to be the proud brother for my sister's wedding to Dr. Kenneth Gale, surgeon and naval officer. After the reception at LaFayette Country Club, I headed back. In the end, I had hitchhiked, taken trains for over a thousand miles each way, and made it back to base, while missing only one roll call formation (Monday morning). Soon after my return, a court-martial found me guilty of the horrible crime of attending my sister's wedding in June of 1944, and docked me three days' pay. The loss of pay for my "crime" of loving my sister was the magnificent sum of $5.00.

The captain was appalled at the unmitigated gall of a soldier whose legitimate request he had arbitrarily turned down, and then illegally exceeded the formal court decision by adding the ignominy of making me clean the latrines for a week.

---

[6] AWOL is an acronym for "absent without leave", meaning to be absent without permission. Spoken as "A-wall" or "A.W.O.L."

Image 6: Photo from My Sister's Wedding

Eventually, the commanding general of the hard-pressed Third Army (George Patton) must have found out about us: we were put on alert status. The 87th Division re-called all of the personnel who were attending special schools at bases all over the southeast, in order to bring us up to full strength as required by the alert.

The time had finally come when we were to be sent overseas. As it turned out, our captain was a first sergeant left over from World War I. For twenty years, he had reenlisted in successive hitches. When World War II began, he was automatically promoted, and because of his years of service, went from administrative master sergeant to captain, landing him in full command of our combat outfit, Company A. But even though he had attended one school after another for decades, he hadn't learned a goddamn thing.

Without any prior combat or command, he was now the leader of our 157-man Company, and it was time for us to head off to war.

Chapter 3: *Queen Elizabeth* to Cobblestones

Image 7: The *RMS Queen Elizabeth*

We took a troop train to the west bank of the Hudson River (Hoboken, NJ) and a ferry boat to the ship that finally took us overseas. The *RMS Queen Elizabeth*[7] was still being built in England when the war started in 1939. It had been fitted with engines and everything to make it go and had been formally launched, but it was far from complete. They sent it directly across to the United States to have the installations completed in the Brooklyn Navy Yard. Had it remained in England, it would surely have been a prime Nazi Luftwaffe[8] bombing target: this great big ship hull sitting at the construction docks in England, just waiting to be destroyed.

Anyone who has ever taken a cruise on a top-of-the-line vessel knows how super deluxe the accommodations can be. Upon completion, the *Queen Elizabeth* was the most luxurious

---

[7] RMS stands for Royal Mail Ship, which was a mark of distinction. For a good overview of her history, see http://rmhh.co.uk/ships/pages/RMS%20Queen%20Elizabeth%201.html.

[8] Luftwaffe means the Nazi air force, from a compound word that literally means 'air weapon'.

ocean liner ever conceived. It was in a class by itself; the décor was exquisite. The Grand Ballroom was lined with mirrors and gilded in gold, and the Dining Room that served as our mess hall was fancier than any of those used by any country's bourgeois elite.

Image 8: The Queen Elizabeth First Class Ballroom

Surprisingly, once we were on the *Elizabeth*, they asked if anybody had newspaper experience. When I said, "Yes!" they made me editor of the ship's paper *The Elizabethan*. The world had been embroiled in warfare since 1939, and radio was the main means of disseminating wartime information. On the *Elizabeth*, we got our news via ship-to-shore radio, which was rare in those days. Every day, my job was to collate, edit, and grind out everything pouring into the ship's radio shack, which was topside next to the Captain's bridge. The news sent to me was heavily censored by the Department of War[9], as were all media, in order to protect our nation's security. It was essential that the morale of our green troops be maintained as they were leaving their native land. It was also critical for them to understand what was going on, and why they were being sent to fight.

---

[9] The Department of War was renamed the Department of Defense in 1949.

The newspaper was to appear on the beautiful dining room tables for the eight shifts necessary to feed our 15,000-man division two times a day. The men would line up outside the "mess hall", and as soon as one shift completed its meal, the next would stream in and be immediately served. The newspaper had to be placed on each table for each shift on each of the five days it took us to make the trip. Over the course of our journey, we printed about 36,000 papers (only one out of every four of our backwoods soldiers could read).

Image 9: The Queen Elizabeth First Class Dining Room

My Special Services quarters were housed in a Princess's suite (the present Queen and her younger sister were children when ship construction started). So there we were, with our newspaper office all decorated with cute little cuddly bunnies on the wallpaper. We were big, macho soldiers breathing in the perfumed air of that pretty little baby's room! It had been pressed into troop ship service and the hand-cranked mimeograph printing machine was sitting on a board covering the sink. The printing supplies were in the towel cabinet, and the paper was kept on a frilly vanity. The assembly line for my thousands of daily copies was in a corridor outside the stateroom. We were printing 'round the clock using unlimited labor resources: thousands of soldiers stuck on a ship with nothing better to do.

Meanwhile, my desk was a card table sitting over her royal Princess's crapper — which served as my executive chair, and is where I wrote the newspaper for those five days.

The good news was that the ship was gorgeous and the weather was uncharacteristically perfect for an Atlantic crossing. The bad news was that the 15,000 men of an entire division were jammed into every nook and cranny. The unfinished staterooms had not yet been fitted with the beds of the rich and famous. Instead, there were stacked hammocks slung from wall to wall, with barely enough space between them to accommodate a soldier's body. Talk about claustrophobia!

Because the *Elizabeth* was faster by far than any other ship on the ocean, there could be no convoy serving us as safety escort. We just zigzagged our way across the ocean to confuse enemy subs. The only way we could be torpedoed was if a Nazi sub accidentally happened to be in our path. As a further precaution, each crossing from either direction varied the landing ports, so that a Nazi sub couldn't conveniently lie in wait and sink a whole Army division in one strike.

I'll never forget when that goof-ball captain of ours gave us a pep talk as we neared the British Isles on the *Queen Elizabeth*. He said, "We're going to land in England, and England is totally destroyed by buzz bombs," (which of course it wasn't), "but people will probably invite you into their (destroyed?) homes to join them for tea and trumpets."

I loved that.

"Crumpets" are what he meant, of course. It was no secret that his commanding officers, down through the years between WWI and WWII, had sent him to whatever away-school they could think of. They didn't want any part of him lousing up training exercises.

It was five days across the Atlantic, and they picked Greenwich, Scotland as our port. We took a train to England and into Stoke-on-Trent (where they make the beautiful pottery, including Wedgwood). From there they had us march to where we were going to stay while in England.

It was a 30-mile walk on cobblestones.

There were no such uneven round-stone roads where we had trained in sandy South Carolina. This was cobblestones, full field packs, and 30 miles. We'd done 30-mile hikes in the States of course, but mostly on sand.

We went a few miles, and guys started dropping out because they were starting to raise blisters. An infantry man is a foot-soldier, and a foot-soldier with blisters is no good to anybody. Finally everybody dropped out. Nobody could make it. We were part of the Third Army commanded by 'Old Blood and Guts' Patton ('his guts and our blood', we used to say), who would certainly not tolerate a mass drop-out on a little old 30-mile jaunt. The orders came back (supposedly from Patton himself) that we were going to do a 30-mile forced march each day on cobblestones with full field pack — till *nobody* dropped out.

We did not just walk around aimlessly. The trucks that followed us onto the cobblestones to pick up the drop-outs trucked us all back to the same starting point every one of those 30 days. This was a smart move, because each of us knew where he had given up to avoid blisters the day before, so it strengthened our resolve to make it a little farther on each successive day.

And for 30 days, that was it. Revelry first thing in the morning, put on full 30-pound field packs, 5-pound sleeping bag, rifle, add bandoliers of ammunition around our waists, and do 30 miles on cobblestones. It took an entire month, but one by one, each of us could make it farther and farther, until finally all of us could make it all the way.

By the end of October 1944, we were tough as nails. When we got done, we were probably the toughest guys in the Army. Our calf muscles were like rock. We were proud of our toughness. We hated Patton while doing it, but ultimately, that extra stamina saved a lot of lives. We were deemed combat-ready.

At the end of that cobblestone march, the place where they had us stay was an old abandoned factory, dating back to the early 1800's Industrial Revolution days. The water-powered belts were still on the pulleys (though rotted out), and it was musty and moldy. The floors were all hand-hewn, as were the roof beams.

Next day, they trucked us to Liverpool, England, and ferried us the 35 miles or so across the English Channel to a prime port of entry: Le Havre, France.

Le Havre was a mess, a total mess. There were no real docks…everything had been completely wrecked by the retreating Nazis, as was their practice. All of the North Sea harbors were likewise destroyed. The only North European deep-water harbor left was the port of Antwerp in Belgium.

We off-loaded from the ferry onto a small LCT (Landing Craft Tank)[10], which brought us to the replacement docks built by the SeaBees Construction Battalions while under fire. That was lucky for us, because usually, LCTs would get you close, drop the ramp, and then you had to wade to shore on your own. Sometimes, soldiers even drowned when they stepped off the ramp into water over their heads while weighted down by all their gear. And those who survived to wade ashore were like ducks in a shooting gallery. This time, though, there were replacement docks. Better than that, there was no enemy. The Nazis had pulled out.

Image 10: Landing Craft Tank

Once in Le Havre, we had to rely on trains for the next leg of the journey. The rail yards were in no better shape than the harbors, having been bombed by us in preparation for D-Day[11].

---

[10] You can think of LCT's as landing crafts for tanks. Their job was to facilitate amphibious assault, and ideally tanks could roll right off their ramps onto shore. Although developed for tank deployment, they were often used to carry men.

[11] Explanation of the term "D-Day": D-Day designates the timing of an upcoming, vital military operation. Using this coded language accomplishes two things: it lets everyone on your own side focus their thinking on the same event, and it does so without widely divulging the details of the actual date. Leaving out these details makes it harder for the enemy to gain this information, and

So every city we went through required lots of time on sidings, as repairs-in-process were making simple through-traffic impossible. Rail yards were easy aerial targets, so they were always totally shot up. We were shunted back and forth to intact parallel sets of tracks, until the train could finally be connected to a useful main line.

Our rail cars were known as "40 and 8's" — WWI remnants marked in French to hold either eight horses or forty men — but cattle cars in either case. There were no seats, and we were so jammed that we rode standing up. Hay covered the floors, and the last loads had obviously been horses, so the "living" conditions for that two-day trip were, politely stated, substandard. Phew!

Image 11: 40 and 8's

allows for flexibility in case of uncooperative weather. Although any invasion can have its own D-Day (the Allies had a number of them throughout World War II), unless other qualified, D-Day refers to June 6, 1944, the day the Allies invaded Normandy from England in WWII. For additional discussion of the term's derivation, including alternate explanations, see the National WWII Museum: http://www.nationalww2museum.org/assets/pdfs/the-meaning-of-dday-fact.pdf.

Out of sheer mercy, they let us out to walk around while we were stopped, and it was there that I first became an interpreter for our Company. My Tennessee hillbilly outfit had very few high school graduates in it, and almost none had come from a school that required at least a year of foreign language before graduating (as my military school did).

French was the first choice at Manlius for a very understandable reason: the young redheaded French teacher was drop-dead gorgeous! She often sat on her desk with legs crossed, which made it very difficult for me to concentrate on the French lessons, and I just squeaked through with a 64 average (65 was passing, and out of the goodness of her heart she passed me).

As inept as I was, I was all those guys had — and it was surprising how much of what little I *did* learn came back to me. The big need for my services was trading US cigarettes for French stuff, foremost of which were fresh-baked baguettes (those long skinny loaves of bread). As we traveled, we lived mostly on boxed, dry K rations. These were cardboard boxes about the size of half of a big book, coated with wax for preservation, and filled with food designed to be eaten at room temperature out of the box. They were the norm for frontline-area vittles. Ah…but I can still taste that great home-made French bread! Later on, my linguistic "talent" was to be much-used as a match-making go-between for love-starved GI's[12].

Four days later, we arrived at Metz, France, carrying our barracks bags. These huge bags held everything we owned except for the front-line field packs that we carried into combat. We'd carried them on a strap over our shoulders with the bottoms nearly scraping the ground…carried, dragged, and schlepped them on foot, on truck, and on ship. On the outskirts of Metz, there was a brick garden wall that they had us line up and lean those heavy bags against. They said, "Wherever you go, whenever you stop fighting, these will be sent up to you so you can have your stuff."

---

[12] GI is an abbreviation for "Government Issue", which characterized nearly everything that soldiers wore, carried, ate, and used. Eventually, it came to stand for the soldiers themselves.

We never again saw what we'd lugged all that way — some of it irreplaceable gifts, mementos, and letters from girlfriends and families.

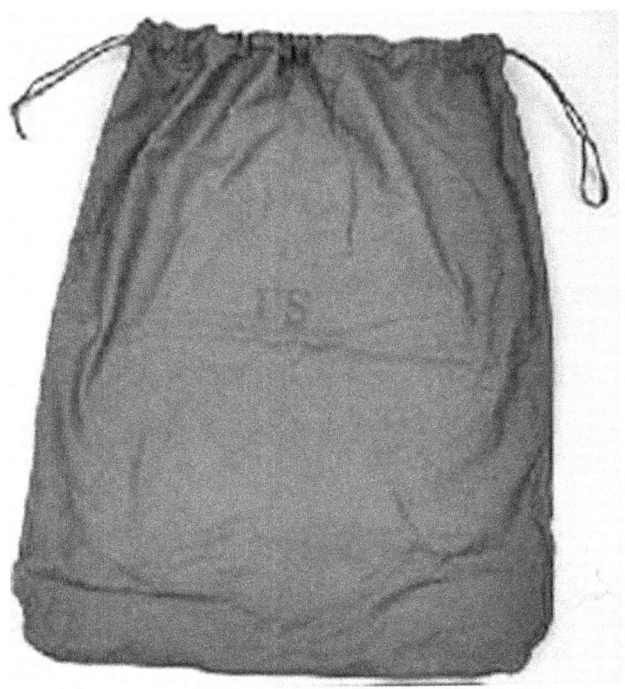

Image 12: Barracks Bag

Chapter 4: Close Calls

Metz, France, was a fortified city. From the time those fortifications were first built in WWI, they had *never* been reduced in *any* battle by frontal attack. No wonder it was invincible: it was all underground, and crisscrossed with tunnels running between forts. First the British, and then the US Third Army continuously threw men against those fortifications; killing a lot of their own, but getting nowhere.

At Metz we were sent to stage a frontal attack on that underground maze, so evidently we were gonna be the next wave to be killed as cannon fodder. We didn't know that, of course. Patton's Third had taken over for Montgomery's British army, which had lost many troops in futile efforts to capture the city. We were all formed up for attack when General Patton (also aptly known as The Great Strategist) decided to bypass Metz and let it die on the vine.

At the last minute, they called off our frontal assault.

Whew! I'm sure God saved my life just then, because attacking Metz was suicide and there was no need for it. We by-passed Metz, and the Nazis inside sat out most of the rest of the war there, waiting for another attack that never came. That Nazi garrison did not surrender and was uselessly occupied until the end of The Battle of the Bulge. No question about it: Patton's decision saved our lives.

The next thing we know, they've trucked us near to the German border, at Nancy, France. We walked through the Maginot Line[13] and headed for the German Siegfried Line, North of Offenburg.

Although we couldn't have known it at the time, we might have been among the first troops to cross into Germany. First or not, since we were crossing over into the homeland of the aggressor, somehow, you'd expect a lot of fanfare.

Instead, there was a whole lot of eerie quiet.

---

[13] Pronounced "MAZH-i-no" (ZH sounded as the z in azure, with a short vowel sound for the i).

The plan was for us to attack a town right on the German border. We arrived there before sunrise to take over from some other division that was being pulled out, and were going to attack this village with flame throwers and all that fancy stuff. Hah! We didn't *have* flame throwers! We were just common infantry. No special weapons, and usually no good air liaison. Never saw planes helping us before, never saw them after, but that day, we had a flight of six Spitfires with British markings and 500-pound bombs under each wing. They were going to soften up that town for us.

Image 13: Spitfire Mark VII

We prepared to attack.

There were concrete pyramids sticking out of the ground as a tank barrier. Beyond the pyramids was a village of thatched roof houses. We walked up to that barrier and stood behind the concrete, calling down the air support. The Six spitfires came in from the west, and dropped their bombs on the houses.

Image 14: Crossing the Siegfried Line

Holy crap! The bombs bounced off!

These "houses" were actually pillboxes[14] that had concrete curved roofs hidden under the thatching. Each "house" also had machine gun slits for the enemy to fire through while being relatively protected. We had no idea that those phony houses were part of the Siegfried Line. We didn't know the fortifications were there, and certainly our commanders didn't. They took one look at those now-exposed pillboxes and they called off our attack. We were totally unprepared for all that concrete. If we had moved forward on foot (which is precisely the

---

[14] Pillbox: a part dug-in, part raised, cement guard-post that is often camouflaged.

infantryman's job), we would have been wiped out. That day was the only air support I ever had in combat, in all the time I was at war, but I can't complain about the timing: those British Spitfires saved our lives!

Twice now, we were gonna take tremendous casualties, and twice they called us off (thank the good Lord). So we went from there…I'm not exactly sure where we were, but it wasn't Germany anymore as we had walked back through The Maginot Line. We weren't ready for a serious move into Germany yet. None of us had any combat experience — none of us on that hill overlooking that fake village. There wasn't any experience in our whole 15,000 man division, except maybe the top guys who might have had experience in World War I. We were green, green, green, green. We had all come to believe that we were merely gonna be *occupation* troops, because why else would we have been hanging around for nine months in the States while the Allies were desperate for frontline manpower?

We had jumped off at 0700…I'm talking November now; it was cold…and a lot of rain…a lot of rain. I remember seeing some foxholes that were full of water, and the other men saying to me, "I don't care *what* the enemy's throwing at me, I'm not gonna jump into that icy water!"

We were about to change our minds real fast.

Chapter 5: Wiped Out on Our First Day of Combat

They trucked us a few miles south of Nancy to replace the 26th Division, which was mostly from Massachusetts. Preparing to engage the enemy, we walked five miles at sundown across rolling, treeless farmland. At sunup, we found ourselves advancing through our own troops in foxholes, as we continued past their current positions. They had been decimated by enemy action while trying to advance over the bald hills.

Now it was our turn.

I was in Company A, which was 157 men. Three of our platoons had 48 men each, and each of those men was a foot-soldier carrying a rifle. There was also a 6-man trench weapons platoon to handle the heavy components and cooperative firing of one trench mortar and two machine guns. In addition to these 150 men, Company A had 1 frontline radio operator and his 2 assistants, 1 company headquarters jeep-mounted radio man, and 3 commanders: captain, first lieutenant, and second lieutenant. Each of the different ranks had identifying insignia[15].

But heading into battle, we wore no shoulder insignia at all. Even the officers wore nothing showing their rank. They didn't want the Nazis to know what outfit we were, or who were officers and who were not. This was standard operating procedure: newly-arrived frontline foot-soldiers were ordered to strip off all identifying emblems and indicators of rank before entering combat, so that the enemy could not gain valuable information just by looking. Green divisions such as we were, coming into battle against the most experienced hi-tech fighting machines in the world (the all-conquering Nazis), would have faced sure death from both the natural bewilderments of poorly-trained men, and by sporting shoulder-patch insignia to shout out who they were. Officers and high-ranking enlisted men wearing bars, oak leaves, or stripes would have been singled out for torturing to reveal their knowledge of battle plans.

Again, we jumped off at 0700. Our three rifle platoons assumed their customary tri-angular formation: two advance platoons side by side at some distance, with the third rifle

---

[15] Our basic combat unit was a squad of 12 men. The squad leader was a buck sergeant (3 stripes), and second in squad command was a corporal (2 stripes). There were four squads, and therefore 48 men, to a rifle platoon. The platoon included a platoon sergeant as commander (3 stripes and 2 rockers), and an assistant platoon sergeant (3 stripes and 1 rocker). Captain's insignia was a double bar; the lieutenants each had a single bar, distinguished from one another by their different colors.

platoon (mine) bringing up the rear as the apex of the triangle. This third platoon was referred to as the platoon in reserve, though in practice, that merely meant being a couple of dozen yards back.

Our two advance platoons went up over the top of the bald hill. Right out of our 25-year old, outdated World War I training manuals, they were right and left in that crazy triangular formation, just exactly right for lining up in enemy gun sights. They were over on the far side, and we were still on the back side, when Nazi artillery came screaming in on the front side. That crazy captain had made it easy for the Nazi gunners — nice, neat geometrically-shaped spreads of cannon fodder. All hell broke loose.

We didn't know (and neither did our stupid captain, though maybe the Army did) that upon retreat, the Nazis zeroed their guns in on the places they'd retreated from. We who were still on the back side of that hill didn't know what carnage was going on. It was front-side stuff, and we were still walking up the hill in our very own nice, triangle-within-a-triangle formation. All we heard were these explosions and a lot of screaming. I remember our platoon sergeant signaling us to stop and hunker down.

I guess my guardian angel was looking out for me, because my cousin, who was close to me in Syracuse (and a couple of years older), had been in the June D-Day landing in Normandy. He wrote me a letter that had chased me for five months before catching up with me. Incredibly, I finally received it in a mail call the day before my first time in combat. He had never written me a letter before, has never written me since (and doesn't even remember writing me that one). But he wrote me a letter right after his Normandy experience, and in it he said, "Dick, I've got one piece of advice for you. Whenever you stop, <u>dig and dig deep</u>." And that phrase, word for word, sticks with me to this day. I said to myself, if my cousin took the trouble to write me — and we never wrote each other before — I'm gonna do what he said.

So there we were. Stopped, and me with my Cousin Bud Pierson's letter in my pocket. Everyone around me was taking his field pack off, sitting on it, and lighting up a cigarette. I never did smoke, so smoking wouldn't have appealed to me anyway. I pulled the shovel out of my pack and started to dig a foxhole like I was taught by the one instructor who had had combat experience in WWI: you dig it in the shape of your body about a foot or two deep, then after that, if there was time, you could expand it.

I'd just about gotten the thing dug in the shape of my body when the Nazi artillery that had been directed on the front part of the hill moved their aim to the back side.

Had we already been combat-wise, we would have known better, but this was all new to us. The guys in my platoon were all sitting up there on their packs, and I threw myself into my foxhole. The shells were raining down and exploding into sharp horizontally-flying metal pieces that are known as shrapnel. Every piece is a different size, so they all make a different noise, "zzz-zzz, whizz-zzz, zzz-zwanggg", flying over me. Finally the artillery stopped and I stuck my head up out of the foxhole.

Nothing but carnage all around me.

Nobody else had thought to dig a hole. They were out in the open on that treeless terrain intended for grazing cattle. All around, guys moaning and groaning, and some were obviously dead. Most were teenagers, with many calling, "Mamma!... Mamma!... Mamma!… Medic!..."

The guy next to me looked like he was all right. He was lying face up and I said, "Come on, Whatever-His-Name-Was, dig yourself a hole." I lifted his head, and I looked, and there was a square hole in the center of his helmet…a perfect square where a piece of shrapnel had hit. When I turned him over, the back of his brains was just blown away. But when first I looked at him, he was just so peaceful and everything.

My whole compact 12-man squad area was strewn with 12 dead and wounded, including a non-squad dead medic…all being viewed by uninjured me. My corporal and my PFC[16] were among the dead. Later, I was a part of other killing fields, but none remembered with such detail as this, my first one.

My platoon sergeant was OK. Maybe he was uninjured because as our leader, he was closest to the brow of the hill when the Nazis shelled the backside. Running bent over, he went from squad-area to squad-area, saying, "See that farm house down there in that small patch of woods on our left flank? We'll meet there at 1900 hours. Meanwhile, stay where you are." I said, OK, and started digging in deep as my cousin had advised. After all, his advice had saved my life once, and my mamma had raised no dummies!

---

[16] Private First Class.

But the Nazi artillery started in on the front of the hill again, and standing up to dig once more seemed like a bad idea[17]. Looking around, I spotted a great big dung mound just a few yards ahead of my foxhole. It was fresh cow shit that the French farmer had piled up to fertilize these hills of his for next spring's crop. It stunk to high heaven! My foxhole not being any deeper than it first was, and thinking there might be more Nazi artillery shells pouring in soon (there were), I just burrowed into that dung mound. About ten inches or so of dung was a good shrapnel-stopper and easier to dig into than dirt, so I dug right into that shit as far as I needed to, and then I poked up a breathing hole. The field was shelled over and over as I lay in there, and I could hear the shrapnel as it struck against the mound: "Thud! Thud! Thud!"

That's the way I spent the rest of the day. Never saw an enemy, just the results of being on the wrong end of Hitler's artillery fire. I never did see the other side of that hill either. There had to have been at least one Nazi artillery spotter dug in on the forward side of the next hill calling in more fire on anything that moved all that day, and anybody showing himself in daylight would have been a dead man.

A hundred yards forward and to the left was the farmhouse. At what I guessed to be 1900 hours that night, I went down to that wrecked house and there were six other guys there, including the sergeant.

"We're gonna have a meeting?" I asked.

"Yeah," the sergeant said.

"Where's the rest of the Company?" I asked, so far seeing only the seven of us.

"This *is* the Company."

Four words. "This *is* the Company." And up until that very moment I was too dumb to be scared. I remember feeling sort of protected and being aware of strange feelings (like trusting my life to a dung mound), yet I wasn't scared. But when he said those four words, fear shot right through me. From that moment on, whenever I was in danger of being shot at, I was *always* scared, which is a good way to be…adrenalin pumping and brain alert.

---

[17] Periodically, the big artillery cannons were allowed to cool off, because they lost accuracy when overheated. As regular infantrymen, we wouldn't know how long this respite would be. There were too many factors to account for, including ambient temperature.

That buck sergeant (the only non-com or officer available to command us) was a better leader than our captain could ever be. When he told me about the meeting, I thought he was speaking just for our platoon of 48 men. It turned out that he was speaking for *all* of Company A. From the 157 men we started out with that morning, he hadn't been able to find any functioning man above the rank of corporal. He was the right man in the right place at the right time to make the most of a horrible situation. That sergeant — our platoon sergeant — was normally outranked by Company brass and Company-level sergeants, and equal in rank to the other three platoon sergeants. But, being the highest ranking man still functioning, he was, by default, in command of the operating remnants of Company A that night.

As far as I know, the sergeant had no way to report back to the battalion. I don't think any of the other six functioning men was a radio operator, and I don't think the sergeant knew that I was qualified as one. Anyway, where was the Company radio? That was anybody's guess. I don't think our sergeant had the means or the time to have yet sent out a runner, and I don't think he knew how bad the situation was himself till pretty close to 1900 hours. He must have thought that there were non-coms or officers surviving in the other three platoons.

In any event, any radio operator was supposed to be directly under the control of the captain, and I was probably the only one of the six who had even seen our captain — and then, only accidentally. On my way up that hill, where its back side started, I looked down into what must have been a Nazi artillery spotter's post (or somebody's deluxe foxhole). It was deep, deep, and it was concrete-lined. And there my captain was. Top of his helmet and overcoat was all I could see of him. No way he could have seen ahead, or directed us, or anything else. He had survived, but he wasn't in our company meeting. I suspect that the sergeant didn't know there was such a place as where he had holed up, so he wasn't invited, which was a good thing or that nutty captain would have loused things up for sure. When I passed him way down on the back side of that hill, he was certainly nowhere in a leadership position. He never did return to the Company, but I was yet to be fully rid of him…

It had been raining and gloomy all day long, and dark must have settled in by about 1800 hours, so between 1800 and 1900 is when the totality of the carnage must have first become known to the sergeant. My guess: he figured that not hearing a thing from a whole company would have sent battalion looking for us as soon as dark settled in, or more likely the fighting-forces on both of our flanks would be waiting for dark to send scouts out to see where we were.

There was a little patch of woods right there next to the farmhouse and the sergeant said, "No way we can establish a front. Let's just dig in on the perimeter of this little patch of woods in all directions, and all we'll defend is this patch." There were only the six of us plus him. Seven men weren't going to effectively defend a company-sized front, that's for sure, but at least he had a plan. We dug foxholes per the usual drill: we dug them in the shape of our body and then we started to dig straight down as many feet as each were tall.

Then the water started to seep in.

All of November had been sloppy wet with rain, and the water table was almost up to ground level. The water came up over our shoulders, where it started to freeze. We soon had collars of ice forming around our necks as we stood in our foxholes in the mud. Then, at night came the phosphorous shells, which the Nazis set off to light up the whole area. We had to stay put in our foxholes to avoid either being spotted, or being hit with the phosphorous — which we knew could burn right through our clothing to the bone. The Nazis evidently didn't see us, so no artillery found our little patch of woods.

I know I really stunk. The water in that hole reeked. The combination of peeing and shitting in my pants all day, plus being covered with cow dung, was kind of a fitting final touch to my uncontrollable shivering and overpowering fear.

About midnight, the phosphorous shelling stopped. A few hours later, Red Cross jeeps appeared over the hill, with their headlights blocked to little slits of amber light[18]. The jeeps were loaded with medics, blankets, and stretchers lashed to the struts. We had been found by our own guys! The sergeant had us six privates go out…each teamed with a Red Cross jeep driver (to make up six pairs of stretcher bearers), with the mission to find the surviving wounded. We located them by their cries in the pitch dark, and brought them to the old farmhouse.

---

[18] During war, there was a nighttime, government-enforced lights-out policy for civilians, in order for cities not to betray their locations to enemy bomber planes. This was referred to as blackout. On a battlefield at night, soldiers also kept all lights to a minimum…purely as a matter of survival. See also http://www.merriam-webster.com/dictionary/blackout.

It was raining with sleet mixed in, and I remember there was a railroad track running alongside the wrecked farmhouse. After each retrieval, we'd set the stretcher down crossways on the railroad tracks to keep our injured off the ground. The walking-wounded, who now had us to guide them, followed us in under their own power to have their wounds doused with sulfa powder and bandaged. Then they helped evacuate the others who could walk. The sergeant and jeep drivers did their best for the wounded men whose stretchers we had parked on the railroad tracks. They covered them with blankets, which were immediately soaked through with rain, and stiffened as they froze. The jeeps went back and forth up and down the dirt road leading to the farmhouse: sometimes returning with medics who set to patching up wounds by the light of the feeble headlights or slotted flashlight beams. The sergeant directed traffic and assisted the increasing number of medics who pitched in by grabbing stretcher handles from us, or buoying up the walking wounded stumbling in from both front and back of that hill. Each time we went out, we had new teams with us that we could direct to areas not yet covered. We squeezed out every valuable minute because we knew that any second now, the Nazis could light up that killing field with phosphorous shells once again.

Those 30-mile fully-loaded daily hikes back in England surely paid off in the stamina of at least us seven (who, at 1900 hours, were already in a state of zombie-like exhaustion), till we hauled in the last of the groaning and screaming from that Hill of Death just before dawn; 23 hours after we first began.

I'll always vividly remember that evacuation run when we had found every living wounded we could locate, and now it was just a case of getting the last few out. A WWII jeep has a set of crossbars on top to hold the canvas roof, but there were no tops on these. The medics would put two stretchers on the crossbars, and then have one of us sit on the front of the jeep and one of us on the back. We grasped one hand around the outside rod of each pair of handles, and started back in a different direction from which we had tried to advance. We were riding up over the top of the left-flank hill, when we heard machinegun fire…"rat-a-tat-tat-tat!" all around us. I thought *Oh, my God, this is the end!* And — probably more by reflex than heroics — we hung on to those stretcher handles for dear life.

It turned out that the machine gun fire was only the sound of the tire chains smacking the underside of the fenders! Not digging in like on the upgrade, they were free to make a racket that scared us out of our wits.

We were led to an aid station (a big commandeered French farmhouse), and we unloaded the two men we were carrying on that last load. The station was full of our guys, but it still belonged to the 26th Infantry Division with their doctors. (Later on when I came back to live in Syracuse and set up civilian life, my father's doctor also became my doctor, and it turns out that *he* was one of the doctors in that aid station at the time. How's that for a small world? The 26th was a Massachusetts outfit; Syracuse is not far from Massachusetts, and they grabbed doctors wherever they could.)

We were a full strength company of 157 men that morning, not one soldier of which had any combat experience going in. I don't know how many of us died, or were wounded, or were missing in action, but only seven of us remained in the ruined farmhouse that night just a dozen hours later. We were no contest for the artillery fire from the big Nazi guns five miles back. Though we never saw one Nazi, we still got wiped out. This was the one and only day I ever fought for the 87th Golden Acorn Division, but I'll never forget those other kids and men who put everything on the line in a November killing field near Nancy, France.

When we finally got all of the men to the aid station, day was dawning. We were shaking and shivering and freezing. It had been a miserably wet and icy night, but no more Nazi phosphorus shells went up (thank The Lord). We got everybody we thought we could find alive, but I have no idea how many dead or quietly dying we left behind…

Seven years after these events, I named my first daughter after that French city — to grace both the innocents who there left the world, and the healing promise of our baby's new arrival into it.

Chapter 6: Your Feet's Too Big![19]

The shoes were frozen to our feet and had to be cut off, along with our puttees, which were those dumb things that lace up from your ankles to your thighs that were all they had in WWI and for most of WWII. Over those in mud and snow you wore *overshoes*, which was ridiculous when compared to the more modern WWII combat boots.

Image 15: WWII Leggings and Shoes

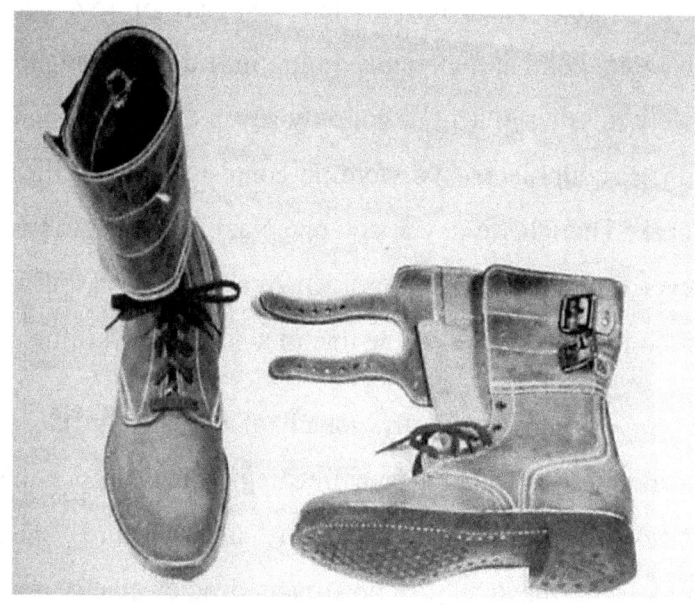

Image 16: WWII Combat Boots

I was fast asleep, but in order to save us from frostbite and trench foot, the medics had to cut the shoes off all seven of us, fast. Luckily, my feet weren't yet frostbitten. A foot soldier's feet are a critical asset to a fighting unit, and those medics knew it. And an infantryman's shoes had to fit, or he soon became a blistered liability.

After we woke up, they said to us, "Here in this corner is a whole bunch of clothing and gear from men who have been evacuated. None dry from your own people yet, just 26th Division guys. Pick a pair that fits you."

---

[19] Chapter title taken from the famous Fats Waller tune of the 1930's.

We helped ourselves, and the other guys were re-equipped with footwear and other stuff that the medics had taken from evacuated or dead soldiers. But, I wore a size 11-quadruple-E shoe, which in those days was big, and I couldn't find a pair to fit me. All I had in footwear was a pair of overshoes and the only size I could get into lengthwise was much too big height-wise when worn directly over socks. There were Nazi blankets that they had been cutting up for various things, so I cut makeshift innersoles from several layers of blanket to pad out the bottoms. I had to make those overshoes walkable, because all the dirt roads had been churned to mud by tanks and trucks, and then frozen into an endless series of bumps. It was like walking on cobblestones again, and my makeshift overshoe padding softened it somewhat.

Combat boots were being issued it seems, but I never saw a pair in combat. I guess combat boots were only for rear echelon guys with influence. I found out later all the guys in Paris HQ[20] were walking around with them. But for the frontline guys, combat boots didn't get that far. Rear echelon guys snatched them from the supply line which was really a criminal thing to do. So we were stuck with those old fashioned World War I type shoes and overshoes. Boots were just part of a bunch of improvements we didn't get (and which, later on we resented when we found out about all the greediness that was going on). Anyway, each day I had to stay in the aid station and look at the shoes of new wounded or dead guys and nobody was my shoe size. The medics supply sergeant had put in a requisition for size 11-quadruple-E shoes for me, but none came. At the end of four or five days they said, "Well, Private Arnold, we don't have the shoes and we're closing this aid station, but we're gonna send you up to your outfit and they'll requisition a pair for you there."

The other six guys from my now defunct battle Company had found shoes and gone on to re-assignment elsewhere in our division. There were a few other combat-fit guys who had come in after us, and the aid station officer said to us "Walk up this road and you'll find your unit." I said, "Wait, I don't have shoes on. This frozen dirt hurts!" He said, "Well, walk as far as you can, and when you can't walk any farther, drop out and there'll be an MP[21] jeep following along, and they'll pick you up." So I said, "OK." and started walking with the rest of the guys, but pretty soon I couldn't walk any farther. I could feel blisters starting, so I dropped out and waited. An MP jeep came along soon after.

---

[20] HQ stands for Headquarters.
[21] MP stands for Military Police.

"You're under arrest!" they shouted.

"What are you talking about, 'under arrest'?"

"For desertion!"

"The officer at the aid station told me to wait here for you; I don't have any shoes!"

"Oh, OK."

They took me to MP headquarters, and brought me to their captain, who was none other than my old Company A captain, obviously having been relieved of command and reassigned. If I had been his commanding officer, I would certainly have reassigned him to non-combat anyway, after his whole outfit was wiped out. So he was the captain of the MP's, and he had me thrown into the German Prisoner compound. No doubt, my having gone AWOL for my sister's wedding was no help to my military career at just this moment. The Nazis had had that compound for American prisoners; now it was an American compound for non-existent Nazi prisoners. It had barbed wire around it and straw on the ground…and I was the only one in it.

As it turned out, the compound guards were my old 87th Golden Acorn Division marching band guys! They were from the same band that was practicing in the recreation hall back in The States where I was writing my newspaper, and I knew them all. For five or six months I had been in the same building with them; they were practicing in the band and I was drinking Cokes to stay up all night writing a newspaper. I had even picked up one of their saxes once in a while to jam with them. All the while, they had other duties, amongst which was being trained as MP's.

They said, "Dick, we never figured you for a deserter. You, of all people!"

"I didn't desert! I didn't desert!" and I told them what had happened.

"Oh, my God, that stupid asshole!"

In the four days that he'd been their commander they already knew what he was. From that point on they gave me decent treatment, including a sleeping bag. Finally, a day or two later they said: "Hey, Dick, you're not under arrest anymore, and here's a pair of shoes that came for you." My shoes had arrived along with new order papers. So now I was fully shod and ready to go back into combat. The MP's said, "We're gonna drive you up to your outfit." I got into a jeep with two MP's up front and me in the back and went down this road.

I don't know where we went, but we started to hear our own artillery firing, and pretty soon we were where they were firing from, probably five miles from the front lines. As an old experienced veteran of exactly one day and night in combat, I knew that five miles back was a nice safe place to be, never giving a thought to what those two MPs' idea of safety was.

"Uh, Dick," one of them shakily said to me. "We've never been this far forward. Do you think maybe you could walk the rest of the way? All you have to do is go straight on this road and report to Regimental HQ. Here are your papers."

My Company A had been wiped out. It had lasted about nine months until combat day, and then just several hours in a killing field. So now, some other company was to be my new home.

I wondered how long *that* was going to last…

Chapter 7: Battle with No End in Sight

Sure enough, a couple of miles down the road I came to battalion headquarters. My file revealed to the Regimental HQ sergeant that I was a graduate of Radio School while stationed at Fort Jackson. That led directly to my star-crossed career as a frontline combat radio-operator. They took my papers and a runner led me down to where Company L was getting ready to jump off the next morning. He introduced me to our captain with the words "Here's your radio operator." I threw him a salute, and mumbled "I'm no radio operator. I haven't touched a radio in maybe six months. All I had was a three-week course. I'm not a real whiz at Morse Code."

"Well, that's three weeks more than anyone else around here, so you're it!

"You'll join my Company L Headquarters staff. Here's our 'Sending in the Clear' code book. Learn it between now and dark. We don't use Morse Code."

He found me two Assistant Radio Operators (ARO's), and introduced them to me. "You've got these two guys under you, so when we get around to doing the paper work, you'll be promoted to Private First Class."

Wow! Think of it. Two years in military school and a full year in the Army, and now, just like that, I've got my first (and only) promotion: from Private to Private First Class. That rank gave me the "command status" from which, on orders from the company commanders, I appointed over a dozen ARO's over the next two months. None of them had radio training in the States, so you try to train them as much as you can in case you get shot, but their main job is to carry spare batteries. Each of those two big, strong riflemen has to lug either two heavy batteries (when I'm using and carrying the even heavier radio-plus-battery rig for transmitting or receiving), or trade me his batteries for the radio (when I'm not actually transmitting). Without rotating in this way, the radio operator would soon be worn to a frazzle. Sadly, I lost half a dozen ARO's — each dying in my stead while carrying the radio while I was not using it. Another half-dozen were wounded — but lived to see their Purple Hearts. My guardian angel was once again at work saving me. Nothing happens by coincidence.

I memorized the codebook, burned it, and joined Company L to replace another company in the front lines.

We were led in pitch dark to a foxhole, but I was wherever the captain parked the jeep, so I got to know those new guys. Nobody envied me my job. Frontline radio operators had a very high rate of death because in those days the radio (weighing 60 pounds with the batteries in it!) had an eight-foot antenna sticking up in the air six to seven feet above you. No transistors or digital circuits. Lots of radio tubes. No plastics. Lots of metal. Meanwhile, that antenna was waving and saying to the enemy, *"Here I am. I'm the radio operator. Shoot me first...then this Company will be isolated from Battalion and the captain can't call in reserves or support from air or artillery."*

The only weight concession helping me reduce my additional load from what riflemen around me carried was the particular rifle I was assigned. Instead of an M-1 rifle, I had an M-1 carbine, which was three pounds lighter.

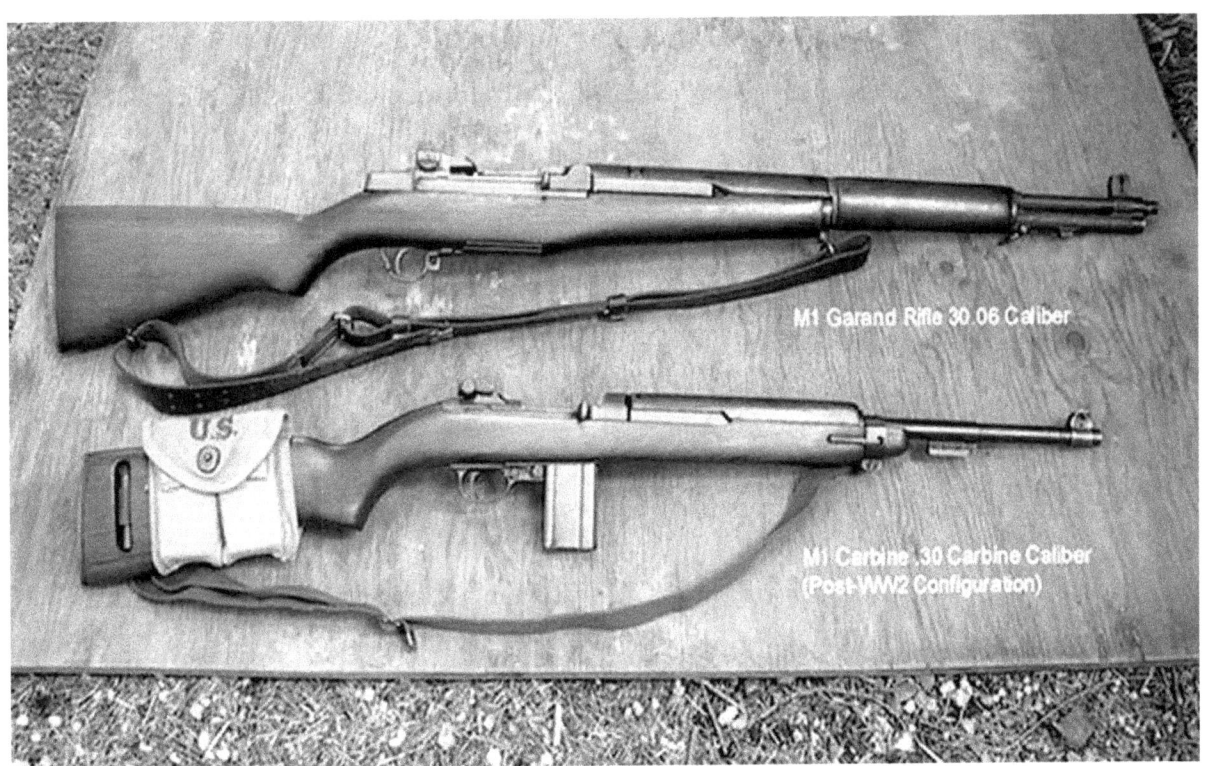

Image 17: M-1 Rifle and M1 Carbine

Well, you can imagine with that training on the cobblestones and all that basic training and now carrying a radio, I'd become a pretty strong guy. One of the things that made me radio operator material was that I was all muscle at 200 pounds and 6 feet tall, which was tall in those days. I'd stand in formation and all the guys around me would be shorter. I was tall and strong and young and healthy, and those are great qualifications for a WWII field radio operator. You have to be articulate, too. Say what you mean quickly and get off the air, because the longer your radio is on, the more time the enemy has to zero in on your location. Those are some reasons why they sent me to radio school — they couldn't send small guys or poor communicators. I was carrying a 60-pound radio plus full field pack, a carbine, food rations, hand grenades and a steel helmet. About 90 strapped-on pounds; walking in mud and later snow and ice. Such was the glamorous life of a frontline radio operator.

Some unique details of this time period still stand out in my mind today. One of the first L Company combat actions I remember was creeping up in the middle of the night to replace an outfit that was dug in…in a graveyard.

Tombstones are great protection from rifle fire, so I could understand why the outfit we replaced picked it as a stopping place. Indeed, we would later see by daylight that a lot of the tombstones were tipped or knocked flat, so it was obvious that the artillery (probably both ours and theirs) had plastered the place — first as the Nazis were pushed back, and then later as our troops fought their way in.

The men we relieved were exhausted by combat and very glad to see us. In those chaotic days when guys were replaced in the front line, they weren't anticipating a rest. They knew they were going to be mighty busy retro-fitting and regrouping around the best of the survivors, who would be getting well-earned battlefield promotions in that period. Some outfits had as much as three hundred percent turnover of frontline troops by the time the European war was over. That was certainly true of radio operators.

In the field, "Company Headquarters" is just a fancy name for a handful of guys usually dug into foxholes near the company commander's foxhole — his staff shooting at the enemy and getting shot at, just like everybody else. Nine times in ten, headquarters was dug in just behind the same ground as the other GI's. Fancy tents were strictly for the movies: commanders had to be up-front to follow the action). This is where the frontline combat radio operator worked….dug in, in the ground. That time of year, (especially THAT year) all over northern Europe it was mud and slime. Once in a while though, Company Headquarters would hit it lucky for a day or two. This was one of those times.

When you replace an outfit in the night, someone from the old outfit leads you to the spot he is leaving. Someone led us down some stairs, and then went back up and pulled the blackout material over the opening. We (the Captain and his staff) found ourselves in a nice dry, safe, *burial crypt* under an above-ground mausoleum. Down those steps there were forty burial spots, twenty on each side of a short ten foot wide aisle: four useable holes high by five holes long on each side of you. A couple of these just had pine caskets in them, smelling of formaldehyde (obviously civilian casualties from the close-by bitter fighting). Most of the others were closed off with granite slabs, telling who died there and in what year…normal gravestone stuff (but in French). A couple of them were bricked up without slabs on them, probably recent deaths in the family, and unconnected to the current actions.

But some were still empty.

The way we took turns sleeping was, you got into your sleeping bag and the other guys picked you up and slid you feet-first into one of the empty holes — an unforgettable experience. Those not sleeping sat on "chairs" made of chunks of destroyed tombstones set across bricks dragged in from the nearby rubble. Across the back of that aisle, the Captain had a map-table make-shifted from fragments of tombstone and bricks. My radio was set sideways on the second-from-the-top step so that the aerial could poke up above the ground level. Radio reception on those old field sets was strictly line-of-sight.

The next morning, because my radio and I were closest to the doorway, the captain said "Private Arnold, go out and look around." I pushed back the makeshift blackout material. Because it had still been dark when we came in, I had no clue as to what our surroundings looked like. All I knew was that we were in the midst of a graveyard. The doors were pulled back; one was awry on its hinges.

I looked, and right smack in front of me was a monastery.

This graveyard was part of a monastery, which was logical. The monastery was three stories high and the wall that I should have been looking at had been blown off by artillery fire. It was brick-on-top-of-brick construction, with no reinforcing rebar. When a wall like that gets hit, it usually collapses in a heap. The building was intact, except for that front wall, which had disintegrated into a pile of brick rubble. Now exposed to my view, was what they call the cells that the monks lived in. They were three stories high and ten across, and each one was identical. Each had a bed and the prie-dieu, where monks would kneel at the foot of the bed to pray.

Looking straight at me were thirty images of Christ hanging from the cross, with thorns around his head and everything. I was absolutely struck dumb. I'd been a very consistent temple-goer as a Jewish boy, and all of a sudden emerging from a crypt in the midst of a carnage-filled war, I'm confronted with 30 images of Christ — the daily inspiration of 30 peace-loving monks. On the spot, I converted — bang! I can't tell you the impact it had. Enormous. Suddenly, being Jewish did not preclude my accepting Jesus as my personal Savior. Talk about baptism by fire.

They say there are no atheists in foxholes. That figuratively means that you do a lot of thinking about your relationship to God (for I never was an atheist). Looking back on that moment, I knew that I had had hundreds of hours of high-stress foxhole thinking leading up to that conversion. It wasn't all that spontaneous. Yet, my moment of ultimate truth was surely that precise moment in time. My understanding of just how it meshed with my Judaism was yet to come, much of it in the events then just months away.

Each of those identical cells had a coal stove connected to a stovepipe sticking out of the wall opposite to where the collapsed side had been. I don't know where we were, but it was in France somewhere east of Nancy. The captain said, "Private Arnold and Private So-and-So, go get one of those stoves. We want to heat this crypt that we're in." So we went up and got one of the stoves, and rigged up stovepipe using joints from other stoves and ran the pipe up the steps from the crypt, making sure that when the pipe heated up it would by-pass my radio without scorching it. You didn't light the stove in the day time when the smoke would give your position away, but at night we lit it and we were nice and warm and comfy, and that's where we stayed. We didn't do any advancing or anything, just occupied that position for a couple of days.

I think that no oral history of war should overlook what fighting men think about in the long, lonely hours between ferocious battles. Especially about God and why He put us in such frightening situations. In those days in that consecrated place, my relationship with God matured. I had plenty of time to internalize my acceptance of Jesus in my life. I began to see that man's communion with God was a continuum. God didn't stop talking with man at the end of the Old Testament; He just started talking through His Son, who carried The Word forward. He still talks with us today and always will. It all has to do with 'Nothing happens by coincidence'. God has a plan that includes all of us. We won't be around to see it, but The Plan will come to fruition when the prayer in my father's Hebrew Union Prayer book is fulfilled:

"Fervently we pray that The Day will come when all peoples will know that to Thee alone every knee will bend and every tongue give homage. When superstition will no longer enslave the mind, nor idolatry blind the eye. Then shall Thy Kingdom be established on Earth and the Prayer of Thine Ancient Seer be fulfilled: On that day The Lord will be One, and His Name will be One."

* * * * * * * *

From November 29 to December 13, 1944, we experienced continuous miserable each-day-the-same-as-the-day-before combat without let-up. I was combat-wise, but the rookie replacements weren't. They were 18-year-old men-boys; woefully unprepared cannon fodder here to replace each day's dead, seriously wounded, and post-traumatic mentally disabled. A huge percentage of those who were trucked in to us each night by blackout-equipped, slotted-headlight jeeps were carried out in body bags by the same jeeps that were bringing in *their* replacements the next night. All that the parents of these men got as a keepsake from their 18–20 years of life together was a Purple Heart, which the government sent to them in the mail.

There is really no need to detail much of the fighting I was involved in during the rest of November and on into mid-December. Most of those days are blurred into one in my mind. We had no days off. Trench foot and pneumonia were our constant companions. General Ike Eisenhower had predicted that the war in Europe would be over by Christmas, and his commanders were pressing on. It was a race to see who would be in Berlin first, and Patton for one, meant to win that competition, no matter how many of us would be burnt out in the process.

Each day was punctuated by death and destruction amid ice and mud and cold with huge amounts of fear mixed in. We fought primarily in the fields and small villages with very little hand-to-hand combat. Casualties from the day before were replaced by green newbies brought in the next night. We never did learn each other's names and I have no surviving buddies that I know of. Boys like myself of the high school classes of 1943 and '44 passed in and out of the range of my radio waves on a daily basis. There was no time to lay telephone land lines. The chain of command was dependent upon runners and radio men.

The Nazis, who had fought an evil war for world conquest on the soil of *other* nations for over five years, were now on the brink of defending their own Sacred Fatherland for the first time. Every mile was bitterly contested. The front line was greatly shortened by neutral Switzerland on the south and the Baltic Sea on the north. As the distance was compressed, so was its defensibility intensified. It was one desperate campaign, rather than a series of battles. And especially challenging to the Allies, sustaining this front required supply-lines *thousands* of miles deep.

Amidst this blur of days, there is one more that will stand out in my mind forever.

The Army wasn't desegregated until after World War II. For me, that meant there was plenty of time to be astonished by both the policies and frank racism that were manifest even in the midst of a world war. When my sisters and I were kids, America's heartfelt racism never made sense to any of us. Once I reached the ripe old age of 10, I had an additional reason to be colorblind: by then, I was nuts for music, especially big band jazz — from Benny Goodman to Duke Ellington. Surely racism, which made no sense in peace time, was pure idiocy during WWII. At various times, African-Americans were not allowed in the military, or not allowed to serve on the front lines. Federal law did not permit them to serve alongside white troops.

Unbelievably, many African-Americans stepped up anyway, to serve as volunteers for their country in World War II. I am aware that there was eventually one black tank battalion, the 761st.

Image 18: US 761st Tank Battalion Insignia

Their web site[22] explains that they were an experiment comprising mostly black soldiers (some of its top officers were white, with some of these mutually respecting of, and respected by, the black men). Nicknamed after their distinctive insignia, all men of the 761st were known as the Black Panthers[23].

But if the web had to remind me that the 761st was an experiment, no one has to remind me of their courage and effectiveness. Company L was in deep trouble. We were advancing through managed forest land, and lots of rain had fallen. The going was slippery and tough for us foot soldiers. What else was new?

The rain stopped, the low-hanging bank of fog made for poor visibility, and the advantage of the killing field once again belonged to the Nazis.

Then came the sound of hope: the clinking and clanking of medium-sized tanks which, therefore, we knew had to be ours. Sure enough, it was a couple of Shermans. One of them turned into the patch of trees where we were pinned down.

The safe thing for a Sherman spotter to do was to call out aiming instructions based on what little he could see through the narrow slits in the tank's belly armor. But with resources thin, visibility poor, and the conviction that he had to get it right the first time, the young black tank commander didn't do the safe thing. He did the effective thing: he stood up through the open hatch for a better view of the target, and successfully guided his gunner. That decision both saved our lives and cost him his, when a round of enemy fire bisected him mid-torso, right in front of my eyes.

---

[22] http://www.761st.com/. See also http://www.tellingstories.org/liberators/fdade/. Be sure to visit at least page 5 of Floyd Dade Jr.'s interview transcript. Click on any paragraph that you want to hear spoken by Mr. Dade himself. To read about other WWII black American heroes not with a tank battalion, consider starting with http://lwfaah.net/people/ltfox.htm or http://www.bjmjr.net/2221/home.htm.

[23] Other units such as the 66th Infantry Division were also known as Black Panthers. They used their own version of a Black Panther insignia, and have their own stories of heroism (http://www.lonesentry.com/gi_stories_booklets/66thinfantry/index.html).

Image 19: M4 Sherman Tanks

Chapter 8: The Surprise of the Ardennes Forest

On December 14, 1944, they trucked us to behind the German-American lines in France, all the way down South of Luxembourg to Stiring-Wendel…south of Saarbrucken, Germany. At just that time, there was a bad weather snap that enabled a surprise Nazi breakout in the Ardennes Forest. Hitler had miraculously hidden 1,100 tanks along with hundreds of other vehicles and men for his breakout. Over a *thousand* behemoth tanks, and somehow our vaunted Intelligence Operatives had failed to spot them. We hadn't a clue.

Hitler's Ardennes offensive that night of December 15–16 was aimed at the Belgian deep water Port of Antwerp, which was the only one of all of the North Sea ports the retreating Nazis had somehow neglected to destroy. All Allied supplies for finishing off the war were coming through that port, and Hitler's objective of destroying it (even temporarily) would have given him weeks and perhaps months to develop the atom bomb ahead of us. Back in MIT over a year later in one of my classes, at my request because of my specific interest in Hitler's Antwerp thrust, we studied how close the Nazi's Heavy Water Project in Norway was to an operational atomic bomb. With the advantage of 20/20 hindsight, class and instructor concluded that Hitler was just a handful of months away, as were we. It was nip-and-tuck. His well-timed, totally secret thrust of tremendous force was favored with eight days of rotten visibility, due to the blizzard conditions that his meteorologists had correctly predicted.

For those eight days, the Nazi truck convoys supplying Hitler's breakout were moving almost unopposed. They were supplying his full-strength tank and infantry divisions that were driving through our thinly-held, overstretched defenses. His Ardennes Forest sector (and in fact the whole of Hitler's Europe) was in no danger from our Allied Air forces: no planes were able to see the ground, and there were no high-tech alternatives as there are today. As Hitler's forces emerged from the forest and advanced through rolling, frozen, treeless farmland, those truck convoys were the lifelines that kept them going (see Image 27).

Unlike tanks and men, trucks were limited to roads. At one small Belgian village, all the roads in that breakthrough area converged before spreading out again a mile later. That village:

Bastogne[24]. The distance in miles between Antwerp (a major city whose population swelled to over four hundred thousand after the liberation) and Bastogne was one hundred and twenty five miles. At tanks speeds of 35 mph, it was a mere four hours away. Only one thing stood in Hitler's way: the American 101st Airborne Division called The Screaming Eagles, after their patch symbol.

Image 20: US 101st Airborne Division Patch

They had been fortuitously air-dropped into Bastogne just before Hitler's huge advantage (bad weather), had socked-in that whole area. That small air-dropped ground force of determined Band of Brothers[25] Paratroopers was holding up the Nazi dream of pure Aryan world domination. Likely, as few as *one* such tank crashing through would have been enough to consume the tenuous resources of the 101st Airborne's ammunition-starved and out-gunned resistance.

The Nazis had to make sure there were no more air drops to support Bastogne. Hitler had to crush that road-straddling obstruction at all costs. He had the weapon to do it: The King Tiger Tank. He had the golden opportunity to use it: those monsters were right at home in that environment of rolling, treeless hills with no Allied planes, and miserable enemy ground-level visibility. For the Nazi armies, this was a window of opportunity: bad weather unequalled in the history of that part of the world hid their operations.

---

[24] Pronounced "bas-TONE".

[25] See also the multiple award-winning TV miniseries of that name, produced by Steven Spielberg and Tom Hanks.

Image 21: King Tiger Tank

Bastogne's defenders had no weapons at all that could stop a King Tiger tank. Our newest and biggest comparable weapon was the Sherman Tank, which was greatly eclipsed in size, armament, and armor by that new, gigantic mobile-fortress with state-of-the-art modifications added specifically by Porsche in time for first usage in the Ardennes breakout. The Nazi King Tiger Tank joined with Hitler's elite Panzer divisions. With its powerful 88 millimeter gun and almost impenetrable body armor, it was one of the most feared weapons of World War II. Up to the end of the war, the Allies (whose tanks only had 75 millimeter guns) had not introduced any effective means to counter its threat when advancing head-on or fired upon from the rear[26]. Only a Forward Observer (FO) team could destroy it. An FO team was comprised of a lieutenant with high-powered binoculars, and a frontline radio operator. The FO team's job was to give aiming directions to the big guns, which had to be located five miles back from the front line. (No doubt, it had been a Nazi FO team that had led to the wipeout of our Company A on my first day of battle.)

The intrepid strategist and tactician General Patton saw Hitler's King Tiger Tanks' opportunity at Bastogne before Hitler's generals did. Just south of Bastogne, Nazi General Hasso von Manteuffel's Fifth Panzer (*i.e.*, tanks) Army was moving cross-lots west, towards

---

[26] An 88mm gun round is nearly 3.5 inches in diameter; a 75mm round is slightly under 3 inches.

Antwerp. Diverting just a few of those monsters northward into Bastogne would be a piece of cake.

We were in miserable ice and snow conditions. My body swung from total numbness in the constant sub-zero cold, to excruciating pain on the rare nights where we found ourselves paused for shelter in barns along with the neglected, stinking cows of farmers who had wisely fled while armies battled on their properties. Normally a prized respite from the bone-freezing cold, the barns were now too much of a good thing for me. Our "roommates" generated so much heat that my frozen body parts would start to thaw, causing both great swelling and loss of numbness — the combination of which resulted in tremendous pain.

Ironically, the only place I could find relief from my deep-freeze injuries was to go back out and sleep in the numbing snow, safe in my trust that one of the other foot soldiers would awaken me — so that I wouldn't freeze to death in my sleep.

Chapter 9: Saar River Massacre

December 18, 1944.

Company L was assigned the task of crossing the frozen Saar River to become possibly the first Allied troops onto German soil, though of course, we were unaware of it at the time. That successful crossing cost us over 40% of Company L, lost to death or serious injury. The horrendous number of casualties was from having to slip and slide down the exposed, sloping west bank of the frozen River, and then climbing up the more terrain-protected east slope to cross into Germany…in bitter cold weather…on fluffy snow which covered the solid-white river ice…with us dressed in fall *brown* uniforms. (All predictions were that the war in Europe would be over by Christmas.) We stood out against that white, treeless landscape which made us appear like sitting ducks to the Nazi gunners, who were crisply dressed in their white winter garb.

Image 22: The Saar River

That day started out as just another of our bloody, pre-Bulge, foot-slogging days that never seemed to end. But somehow, at the end of that particular ten-hour day, we had crossed the river and gained a foothold on the other side. We were dug in for the night where a Nazi chalet had been destroyed above ground, leaving an intact bomb shelter underneath.

Suddenly, at just after midnight (now December 19th), my radio came to life with orders for my captain to pull us out and *re-cross* the frozen Saar back into France.

Wait a second.

We had just lost over 60 men getting to the German side of that big, frozen River, and *now they wanted us to cross back over our own blood and return to France?*

This may surprise you, but as we passed our own troops and advanced back to the sloping banks, I was not thinking about the waste of that expensive crossing. I was thinking that maybe this give-back-to-the-enemy withdrawal meant I had a better chance of surviving whatever might come next — long enough to celebrate my first Christmas as a Christian.

Around daybreak, we re-boarded the 6x6 trucks that were waiting for us a mile back from the River. We headed north and a bit west up the road. On the way, we were attacked by a single Messerschmitt plane that appeared under the clouds to strafe our convoy.

Image 23: Messerschmitt Bf 109

He hit a few guys in each truck, and those who were not hit jumped over the sides with their rifles, and into the ditches on either side of the road to avoid the next run. The plane circled around again, and everyone shot at it as it passed. Finally, we struck the gas tank, and it blew up into a huge ball of fire. We climbed back into the trucks and handed our wounded down to the Red Cross, who, all the while, were slipping and sliding on the already-frozen new blood.

It turned out that we were headed to Belgium to try to help an obscure, recently liberated European village from falling back into enemy hands. We couldn't know it, but I and at least hundreds of thousands of other innocents otherwise destined to die, were at that moment badly in need of a special miracle. In this one corner of eastern Belgium and small parts of abutting France, Germany, and tiny Luxembourg, there were about a quarter of a million fighting men on the Nazis' side, and again that many fighting on the Allies' side…plus uncounted thousands of avenging newly-liberated locals picking up and firing the weapons of the dead and wounded scattered all around them. That means that well over half a million men were all locked in mortal combat on one front line. Although I had no idea at the time, it was already by that date one of the biggest battles in the history of the world.

Battlefield conditions were chaotic.

I didn't even know what Division I was in. My original Company A of the 87th Division had been wiped out. By the time I was given my first assignment as a frontline radio operator, I was in Company L, but — and this would surprise no one with frontline experience in WWII — I had no idea what battalion of what division that particular Company L belonged to. Remember, we stripped off all identifying shoulder patches and insignia before frontline battle. All I know is that years later, I learned that my division was not the one I had started into combat with a month and a half prior.

All three shot-up divisions pulled from the Saar crossing were extra troops that had been brought in to spearhead the invasion of German soil for the very first time. Ours was one of those three divisions. When that mission was scrapped, we were freed up for other action. The already dug-in American troops simply stayed in their west bank of the Saar river defensive positions and we moved on to Belgium.

On December 20, 1944, the front was just an arc. By the time we arrived on the scene two days later, that arc had been converted to a complete encirclement, facilitated by our forces pulling back on purpose.

Smart tactics.

This forced the enemy infantry laying siege to the village to do battle with our forces from their *rear* at the same time they were trying to penetrate the last-ditch 101st Airborne's defenses holding Bastogne at their *front* (see Image 27). Surrounded on all sides, the 101st's last-moment rescue from the unthinkable options of surrendering to the Nazis or being wiped out, was to come from three tired divisions (including the remainder of ours) of Patton's Third Army, driving up from the south. Patton had accomplished what Twelfth Army Commander General Omar Bradley said was impossible: pivoting us from an eastward-facing front line to northward, rushing us 100 miles in 36 hours, and then hurling us (without rest) into *another* battle, namely the front line at what would later become known as The Battle of the Bulge.

Both sides knew that the US Army's new encirclement was operating totally in enemy territory; there were enemy tank-columns everywhere.

Who was surrounding whom?

Fortunately at the time, von Manteuffel's tanks were following Hitler's orders to drive straight through to Antwerp. Patton foresaw that it was only a matter of minutes or hours before the mastermind Hitler would see what he had already seen: Hitler could have von Manteuffel turn some of his terrible King Tigers on *us*, smashing through our thinly-held US Army outer circle, pass through the Nazi inner circle, and open up the Bastogne-blocked critical supply roads — without which his war machines would grind to a halt. And don't forget that miserable weather with its rotten visibility. It would have been a piece of cake for those tanks to wipe out everything in their path.

At least our forces had great maps of those hills, because the Allies had controlled them just before the Nazis caught us by surprise and grabbed them back. There was one other interesting feature: a rail line running across the southern portion of no-man's-land. The tracks did not go through Bastogne or its southern suburb of Tillet[27], but along the ridgeline south of Tillet on the high ground.

The lieutenant and I watched Tillet's demise as it was pounded into burning rubble (from whose shelling we did not know). We never had a glimpse of Bastogne, which stood just a couple of hills beyond Tillet, but we were nevertheless to play a vital role in its 101st Airborne defenders' immediate future. Earlier on that same day, a Nazi surrender-ultimatum had been hand-delivered and read aloud to the 101st acting commander General Anthony McAuliffe under a white flag. McAuliffe's one-word reply of "NUTS!" (written as a note for the enemy to read) was the much-remembered masterpiece of understatement that came out of WWII. The confused Nazi white-flag surrender team major must have turned to his three accompanying subordinates and asked: "Vas ist das 'Nootz'?" ("What does he mean by 'Nutz'?"). The soldier who hand delivered the reply is reputed to have offered that, in plain English, "NUTS!" means "Go to hell!"

But what we were about to do was all the explanation that Nazi major would ever need.

---

[27] French pronunciation: "till-A".

Chapter 10: From Cut to Fill

Railroad tracks do not go up and down inclines like roads do. If the ground isn't nearly flat, it has to be made that way, if only just where the tracks need to go, as in this part of Belgium. When preparing a rail bed in hilly country, construction crews either have to cut away the top of the hill in their way, or make a cut into the hill and use the dirt from the cut to build up a long strip of land between that cut and the next hill in their way. If they have to blast a cut through rock, the sides are steep; but in the soft dirt in that part of Belgium, those cuts' sides sloped away from track at about thirty degrees. Our single-track roadbed thus traversed a series of cuts and fills, cuts and fills, cuts and fills.

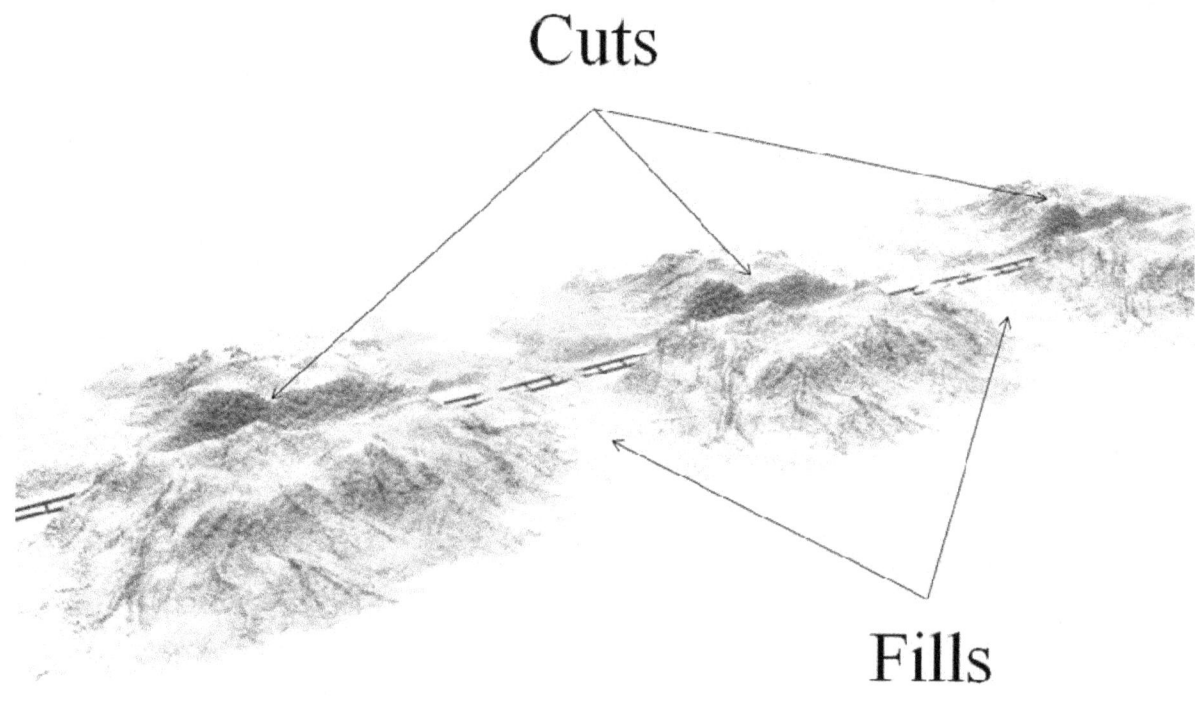

Image 24: Rendering of Cut and Fill Railroad Bed Construction

Where the track lay on a segment of fill, running along it would have exposed us to observation, machine-gun fire, and trench-mortar shelling from the direction of the Nazi troops surrounding Bastogne. Running parallel to the top of the fills just *below* the enemy's line of sight was not possible on those slippery snow- and ice-covered slopes. The *cuts*, on the other hand, formed great protection from enemy ground observation. While you were running through their five foot high corridors, you would not easily be seen by their ground forces to either the north or south. Heading westward in these hills, that railroad followed a rising ridge line. Each successive cut was at a higher elevation than the one before it. Air sightings of us were restricted by the extremely low-lying cloud deck. In this situation, the bad weather favored *our* position. The few Nazi planes still flying would have to take enormous risks to skim close enough to the ground to detect us.

December 21, 1944 started with a bit of luck.

Our blizzard-obscured, virtually invisible convoy of trucks got us near to the railroad's destroyed bridge. No foot-slogging from trucks to fighting grounds as was the usual case. We used the one big cut immediately to our west as a staging area. Fortunately, the enemy had left no troops behind in that cut while pushing ahead to close in on Bastogne. From our convoy's supply truck, I picked up and strapped on my radio; my two ARO's each hefted up on his brawny shoulders (an asset looked for when picking my assistants) his 50-pound, twin-pack of spare batteries, and our captain gave his orders:

1. The company HQ First Lieutenant, second in command to the Captain, was to take me and my two assistants down those tracks to the next cut, and then the next.

2. When we arrived at the first one, I was to report from my radio to the Captain's jeep-mounted radio. I would let him know that the first cut was clear, and advise him what number of men the Lieutenant thought was minimally needed to defend a cut of that length.

3. Then the Captain designated which men were to stay there in that first cut, sent them in to defend it, and sent the rest of the L Company's foot soldiers (badly depleted by the Saar action), through the blizzard on to the next most westward cut, where the four of us were waiting for them.

4. The remaining men ran through the first cut and joined us in the second cut. From there on, the process repeated without involving the Captain. The Lieutenant appointed those who would stay in a cut, after which the four of us would dash across the next fill to the next cut to make certain it was unoccupied by enemy troops. (We four were apparently expendable if it was enemy-occupied — blizzard conditions would have blinded us until it was too late.) All remaining men, on signal, would run to join us, and in each instance a few were appointed to go no farther, and to immediately dig in, to defend their cut. This was to go on until the enemy either challenged us, or just the four of us were left. At that point we would stop, because we would have strung out our men in the cuts behind us.

So we would run out single-file, with the three of us privates stepping in the footprints of our Lieutenant, running onto and across the fill from the west end of each cut. Sometimes one of us bearing the extra weight of radio or batteries broke through the thigh-deep ice crust beneath the heavily-falling snow — spots where the unencumbered Lieutenant leading us had stayed on top. He would then turn around and help that man back up onto the ice (the sooner we all got across the fill to the next cut, the safer we'd all be). Upon arrival, the Lieutenant would clap his gloved hands toward the cut he just left as the signal for "all clear" to those who were to continue on (we couldn't see through the blizzard to the cut we had just left, and yelling might reach enemy ears, but the gloved "clap!" served its purpose well). For those who followed, the going was much easier, as they ran in our footsteps and avoided the breakthrough spots. We would catch our breath while the men following us made it across a fill. Once they arrived, and the Lieutenant determined who would stay, we would fast-walk down the length of the cut, during which time I would call in to the Captain's radio with the code word "Goodnews" that signaled to him that all men not yet deployed had made it safely into yet another cut[28]. We three privates were in superb physical condition, but with all that we had been through (and with such little sleep) since the first crossing of the Saar four days earlier, it amazes me still that we carried all that additional radio-and-batteries-weight (60 pounds for me carrying the radio, 50 pounds for each of the other two)…to which was added our rifles, food, ammo, and grenades, and all the stuff the others carried (about 30 pounds more).

---

[28] Especially with the weight that my ARO's and I were carrying, we fast-walked instead of running in the cuts, because while there, we were relatively protected. To conserve energy, we only ran across the wide-open fills between the cuts where we were exposed.

Finally, we found ourselves with just one last fill to cross by ourselves and we shored up our strength with the thought that we were arriving at last to wherever it was that God had willed us to be. It was mid-afternoon, and we were as yet undetected. The longer those Nazi infantrymen didn't know we were there behind them to their south, the better our chances were. They thought their own forces were slashing westward south of them, which they were. But under the cover of those blizzard-like conditions, we were a brand-new unseen element positioning ourselves between them and their own neighboring not-yet-turned-northward tanks.

Unfortunately, as we started across that last fill, our good luck ran out.

The blizzard momentarily lifted, and an enemy observation point to our north must have spotted us. While we were still three-quarters of the way across (still about 25 yards away from our next cut for safety), a hastily-aimed trench-mortar shell launched against us and fell into our midst. My two assistants and the Lieutenant were badly hit, and a tennis-ball sized chunk of steel hit the stock of my rifle, which slammed flat against my thigh. I could see there was no rending of the cloth over my thigh, so I hoped that I was only badly bruised. A couple of inches up or down either way, and that chunk would have cost me a leg, which, given the weather conditions, would also have cost my life.

I pitched myself over the south side of that fill (away from the mortar operator) and crawled through the snow and ice parallel to, and below, the level of the tracks. I awaited the renewal of the blizzard to crawl back up to where we were hit, and under its cover quickly determined that the other three were dead.

With the possibility that the enemy could even then be sending out a scout to see if more GI's were about, and being much closer to the next fill than the previous, I limped through incredible snow and into whatever haven the cut's sides might offer. The renewed heavy snowfall was quickly covering up all traces of everything. My guardian angel had been once more on duty. As far as I know, no Nazi ever came looking to check us out. Surprising, if true. Our badly-decimated Company L was deployed as planned, and I had my radio with me over which to report and ask for further orders.

Just as I reached the last cut under cover of the renewed blizzard, I saw something that was sure to be either very good news — or very bad: three men I did not know were already occupying "my" last cut. From their fresh footprints in the continuously-falling snow, I could see that they had come in just a few minutes before, running cross-lots in from the south, hidden from view by the extreme blizzard, as we had been. They were wearing American uniforms, but now I had a dilemma. One of the first messages I got over my radio from battalion that day was to warn us that some of the Nazis breaking out of the Ardennes were wearing captured American uniforms, and speaking un-accented English.

"Who's 'The Sultan of Swat?!'" I challenged.

"Babe Ruth!" came the correct reply.

Thank The Lord. We all knew we were the genuine GI article.

We were the tips of two different incursions that Patton was rushing in from east and south simultaneously. That railroad cut was a point of intersection between our outfits. As I was the farthest out from Company L, it is safe to assume that the four of us were the *only* such intersection.

It turned out that these soldiers were the remnants of an FO team sent out to guide an artillery outfit: two fresh, untrained ARO's and their lieutenant, who served as a forward artillery spotter. With his long-range binoculars, he was one of the pairs of eyes for several 155 millimeter cannons (guns so huge that they had to be pulled by slow tractor) — all from some outfit that I never heard of before, or since. When the lieutenant saw the radio on my back he said, "You're a Godsend!"

I didn't dispute him. His own radio operator had obviously never made it to their cut. Before our stumbling into each other, he had lost all communications capability with his big guns five miles to the south of us. And that huge artillery, with no eyes or voice from the front line to guide them, lay useless, silent, and cold. He asked if my radio had the capability of changing channels. I said "Yes," and he immediately pressed me into service to re-establish connection to his big-gunners. If the snow ever cleared, we would be in the right place to view anything coming into Bastogne from the South (*i.e,* the Nazi King Tiger Tanks). He was once again their eyes, and I was about to become his voice, for aiming.

"Call your Company L captain, advise him of the death of his lieutenant and your assistants. Request permission to switch frequencies and be out of touch for as long as a highest priority new assignment makes necessary."

My Captain realized that I was no longer in a position to transmit further useful information about the men. He also realized that whatever we were up to, keeping me on the air for a better explanation was too dangerous. So, he said, "OK."

It was December 1944, and I had been over a year getting here from the time I went into active service. For that whole time of training and re-training in the southern USA, and even in deadly combat as part of Patton's Third Army in France, I felt that whatever I did made no difference in the outcome of the war.

One GI more or less.

At last though, God had brought 19-year-old me into contact with three other men — all in the right place, at the right time to make a material difference.

I had never done anything like calling down live artillery fire, but the lieutenant was a good communicator and I, in civilian life an MIT undergraduate, was a quick learner. Also, the protocol of US armed forces radio communication was universal, so training me was a matter of minutes. Training my two adopted assistants in the basics of being radio operators (in the event I was hit) now became my responsibility. As brand-new green replacements in their artillery outfit, these men had never had the time to become proficient enough to be of any substantive help in the action that was about to take place. I was now taking orders from the lieutenant as his temporary new radio operator.

My rank was Private First Class, just one small step above the two no-rank Privates with whom he had arrived. Thus, because of my exalted rank, the lieutenant had me supervise the digging of a three-man foxhole, off the southern edge of the railroad tracks in the bottom of the cut (see Image 26). Meanwhile he went about taking his next step in setting up shop to search for the enemy, and put them out of business in our sector.

With the aid of his shovel/pick (entrenching tool), he climbed up the sloping south wall inside our cut, and located the best vantage point for his foxhole: near the crest of the slope. He dug in just below its rim, where it and the opposite north slope had a natural dip. This would give him a clear view in both directions, through his high-powered binoculars.

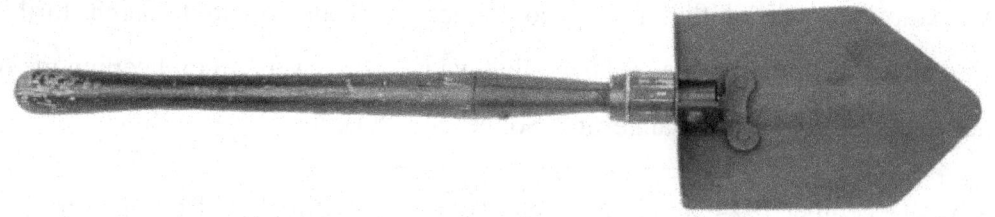

Image 25: WWII USA Entrenching Tool[29]

When our three-man foxhole was finished, I climbed back up to the lieutenant, slipping and sliding, to see where he wanted me to dig my daytime foxhole for working with him. My radio's priority for a best foxhole location was different from the spotter's. In those days our radios transmitted only in line-of-sight. That means if anything were between the tip of my radio's antenna and the tip of the antenna of the radio I was communicating with, the signal would be blocked. For that reason, the antenna was telescopic so it could be extended to eight feet — six feet above my head, and therefore 12 feet from the ground. It was a great feature for the enemy, which is why frontline infantry Company-level radio operators and their assistants had such short life-expectancies.

The lieutenant had me dig my daytime foxhole a few yards west of his, where there was no dip. My ideal position was as high as possible, without letting my antenna extend past the snow and ice ridgeline. If the weather cleared, we must not let that shiny metal present a unique light reflection or we would be found out. To minimize the chance of sound detection by enemy scouts, he would have to whisper to me what he wanted me to radio to his artillery gunners. Because our forces had liberated this railroad track a few weeks before, our spotter had the advantage of newly updated maps, which gave him excellent intelligence about the surrounding wide-open farmland. If the sun ever came out again, he knew exactly where we were, and where we would be operating. To the north, where the side of the cut was much lower, if the weather ever cleared, he would be able to look down into what was left of the town of Tillet, and see the rolling farmland that surrounded the town on all sides. To the south, there would be more rolling farmland. Due east and west, we'd both be able to see right down the railroad bed.

---

[29] Image does not show the pick attachment.

When nighttime came, it would be impossible for my spotter to see moving targets at any distance (nothing was moving anyway), so as dusk fell and I was to be unable to see any longer, I asked for the lieutenant's OK to slide back down to the three-man hole and add my firepower to theirs. During daylight hours they two were to stay in that hole and be our protection from any enemy that might stumble into our cut. At night we became three with the same assignment: protecting the lieutenant. Digging into that ice and solidly frozen rock-like earth was brutal hard work. But all of us were about the same age, 18 to maybe 20, and we had the stamina of youth to get it all done.

Image 26: 3D Rendering of Foxhole Locations

In my nighttime three-man "home" and "classroom" I was supposed to teach my two privates how to operate the radio, and all about the communications codes and radio protocol that I had learned back in The States, and that I had been using in combat the past few weeks. Picture the sight of all three of us standing side-by-side in that foxhole. Each one of us was shivering from contact with biting sub-zero-cold ice and snow. We each also shivered from just plain fear: a fear heightened by pitch-black darkness. Add to the mix our acute suffering from extreme weariness and it can easily be understood why teaching anybody anything was surely doomed from the start.

When I climbed up to my foxhole near the lieutenant the next morning, we decided that it was too risky for me to drag the radio up and down that treacherous slope. From now on, at dusk I would place it beside the lieutenant's foxhole, and if a call came in while I was at the lower foxhole, he could take the call without me. All calls were directed at him anyway. I was primarily a messenger. Breaking a leg climbing with that 60-pound beast up and down the ice-covered slope could threaten the whole artillery mission. Anyway, nothing happened that we could do anything about at night. It was just too darn dark — and then there was the debilitating cold.

God had delivered me as a viable replacement to work under this baby-faced lieutenant. With his regular radio operator dead and their radio smashed, the "coincidence" of my arriving alone and bearing a frequency-tunable radio (not to mention the fact that I theoretically knew how to call down artillery fire from my training in school) can only be ascribed to Divine intercession. Something was up! The lieutenant hadn't lost any time in going about putting things in order for our moment of extraordinary opportunity. He didn't miss a beat. He had me quickly call in our potentially potent situation to his artillery commander.

Not long after getting our act together, over the soundless snows we heard the beginning of muted distant sounds coming from tanks' deep-throated twin engines. This was the beginning moment of my first experience with the much-talked-about, super-huge, Nazi King Tiger Tank.

It is an understatement to say that those faint sounds had our full attention! It was obvious that there were several of them, and they sounded as though they were headed in our direction. But soon, their engine sounds changed. They softened. Idling, maybe. We surmised from our familiarity with our own tanks, that they were fueling up from the jerry cans of gasoline that tanks carried with them and that they were buttoning up against the incredible cold and preparing for the coming dawn, at which time they would rumble on out into the endless snow and fog.

We hunkered down for the most miserable of nights. We were freezing cold, scared, and unable to build a fire for fear of giving away our position. We knew we were in a no-man's-land. With enemy tanks on our south, and enemy infantry on our north, it was not what Christmastime was supposed to be.

With the impending dawn, there were new sounds to interpret. One lone tank was starting to move out first. Its un-muffled huge engines' rumbling was building towards a roar. This was a big one all right! And there was no question that it was headed directly at us. From what started out being just its engines' noises, we began to sort out a new counterpoint harmony: the clinking, clanking sounds of its tank treads laying down their own road as that monster advanced toward us. Surely that unique racket would never stop ratcheting up until it ran me over! While that ominous new cacophony of noises was no joking matter, I remember it incongruously calling to mind "The Wizard of Oz" and how the Wizard described the Tin Man as a glittering, clittering, clanking collection of collagenous junk. In combat, when I was often so totally alone, the ability to make fun mental connections to my previous life, to which I hoped some distant day to return, kept me from long since having been reduced to a basket case.

Fear is the combat soldier's constant companion, and for me it had started six weeks earlier on our first day of combat. In that day's carnage, the sounds of war were all explosives and screams. All that death, and we never even *saw* a Nazi. This approaching monster was something new for me in the sounds of battle that the nightmares from war are made of. And then there are other nightmares, such as that of the near-zero visibility that had been our lot most of the time since December 15th.

When the snowy grayness of dawn arrived, how could we shoot at a monster we couldn't even see…until it was right on top of us?

Then came the miracle of Christmastime 1944.

Chapter 11: Advance of the King Tigers

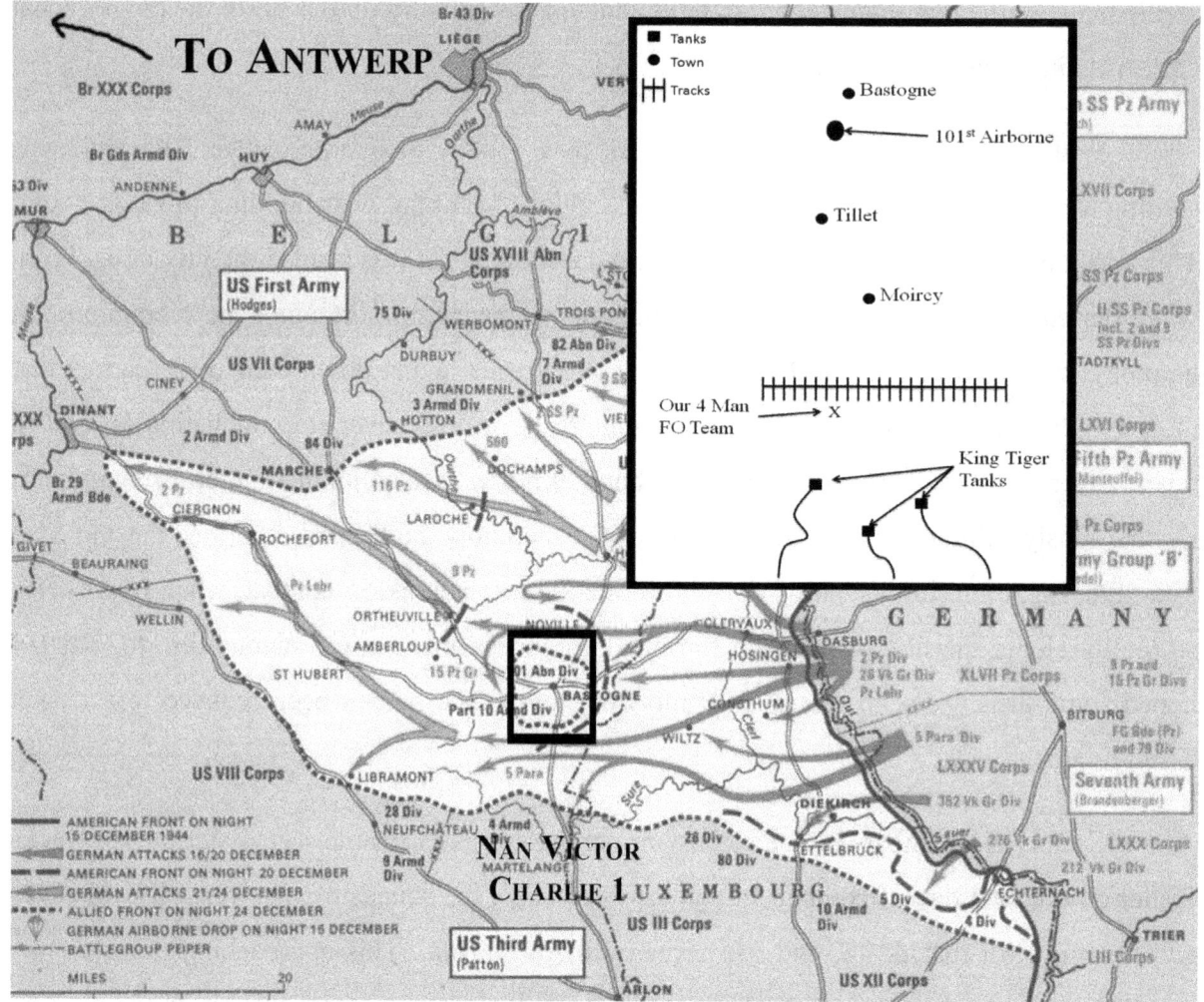

Image 27: Our Position December 24, 1944

On December 24th, the dawn broke clear and shining — and though still murderously cold — we could see! The King Tiger Tanks would come, but at least *we* might see *them* first.

Though it was sixty-six years ago, I remember our call letters like it was yesterday. The artillery group to which we were feeding gunnery directions was Victor Nan Victor. The lieutenant's call letters (and therefore, also temporarily mine) were Nan Victor Charlie One

(NVC-1). He said there was also an NVC-2, (another spotter and radio-man Forward Observation team), and an NVC-3, etc. Our code source-book was *Run, Spot, Run*[30].

As a reminder, the Nazi King Tiger Tank ("The Konigstiger") was new in mid-1944, and by far the world's most fearsome ground weapon. We never had anything that could counter its threat when advancing head-on up close. Our 155 mm[31] heavy guns had a chance, but they were not agile. They were so far back from the front line they couldn't see anything, and had to be aimed by an FO team.

Suddenly, that FO team was *us*, and aiming them was now *our* job!

With his miraculously clear sighting of the lead King Tiger Tank to the south of us, the lieutenant started whispering over to my daytime foxhole the information that I immediately passed on through my radio to his huge guns, somewhere five miles to the south of us.

Our tank hunting mission was on!

That first tank presented huge and black. Operating in fresh-fallen snow, no matter how many hundreds of yards away, as long as it was in our panorama, our spotter could not only see it, but he could also see where each shell we had caused to be fired for location had landed.

As we directed the artillery gunners to zero in on that first King Tiger, their initial shells blasted to one side or the other. The tank driver zig-zagged his evasive maneuvers. But once our locator shells successfully bracketed him on the left and right, the lieutenant whispered to me to tell our big artillery guns to "Fire for effect!"

The lieutenant was amazed by the huge numbers of shells that poured in to our target. The shells would fly in too thick and fast to have come from just the couple of guns normally assigned to Nan Victor Charlie One. He believed that we were possibly the *only* spotter-radio combination that had made it through to our sector from his battalion.

Although the Nazi King Tiger Tank was impenetrable, when hit by our 155 mm heavy guns, its treads were blown off, their lubricating oil ignited, and the resulting heat literally

---

[30] During parts of the War, the code books were linked to the Dick and Jane series of elementary readers. You'd have to know which word, of which line, on which page was that day's code word. You carried both the relevant Dick and Jane book, and the small spiral-bound list of daily "addresses" for the code words within that story book.

[31] At 155mm, each round was over half a foot in diameter.

roasted alive the men inside. When they threw open its three hatches to escape, air rushed in. This created an inside firestorm hot enough to blow up the ammunition, which then ignited their jerry cans of gasoline.

This first tank was the easternmost of those we engaged and destroyed. The lesson its destruction taught its brother tanks was where *not* to strike out across those hills toward Bastogne.

If I remember correctly, the tally marks I scratched in the ice lining of my upper foxhole reached nine the first day and five the second. In any event, at the end of the second day, I saw the total of 14 tanks corroborated by the lieutenant's logbook.

Only nine kills in ten hours of daylight meant that there were often lulls between our actions. Total absence of preliminary engine noises meant that no tanks were on the move. This set me to thinking: the start of the next lull would be our opportunity to do the one last essential thing required to put our business affairs completely in order.

I reminded the lieutenant that if we were going to be in this position very long, my batteries would run out. My recommendation was, at lull times, to recover my spare battery packs. They lay at the bodies of my two Company L assistants, about 30 yards away on that last fill before our cut. Unfortunately for me, those two bodies were surely covered with snow by now, which meant that only I knew where their battery packs were likely to be. I needed to go get them, and to go alone. Taking his other two men with me (all of us in *brown* uniform clothing) would make us far more likely to be spotted…potential disaster.

It also occurred to me that I was setting up a situation whereby, after bringing back the first set of 50-pound batteries over ice and snow, I could leave both my radio and that first set for the lieutenant, and hightail it on back to my own Company. It would be a lot safer than staying where I was and being hunted down by the Nazis, whose prized tanks and golden opportunity for retaking Antwerp were being snatched away by some "Amerikaner schweinhunds"[32] hiding in those hills.

Whatever evil those Nazis were, as Europe's most experienced war-makers, they were no dummies. Finding us would be a matter of minutes, or at the most, hours.

---

[32] An insulting term meaning "pig dog", and pronounced "SCHVINE-hoond".

I could rationalize that I had already gone beyond the call of my Company L duty to help set up the tank-killing scenario as it was, and it was time to get out. I was fully aware of the fact that although my radio was not expendable, I was. A lieutenant in the artillery surely knew how to operate a basic, uncomplicated radio. He could deal with it alone.

Running away in a situation like this was a viable option I had seen other frontline combat GI's take. But I was also aware that if the lieutenant were hit and unable to carry on, I could do *his* job. I had had two years of map reading and artillery theory in school, and just now, had had a few hours of actual in-combat experience where I would be perfectly situated to do big-time damage to the enemy. Nothing like being a part of real-time action vs. hearing about it in a lecture hall or on a drill field. Even as my mind weighed the theoretical possibility of getting back to slightly better safety, I was hoping that the lieutenant already knew me well enough to trust me not to abandon him. I knew in my heart that it was not by coincidence that I was exactly where I needed to be. God had sent me there to *fight*!

So twice, I went dashing out during lulls to search for the battery packs. They were hard to find because not only were they covered in new snow, but they were also covered by the wind-blown drifting and shifting old snows, created by those blizzard conditions of the day before. Our kill count of 14 could easily have been much less without those packs. The intense cold and long time on the air directing fire on each zig-zagging target would certainly have drained my original first set before our job was done, and most probably the second set. (I couldn't be sure of this, because I kept rotating the batteries into the set to give them a chance to bounce back between usages. None were allowed to dip down to where signal strength could be compromised.)

There was one other reason for bringing in those battery-containing packs. They also contained emergency food. We would stuff boxes of K rations in between the batteries and the canvas slings in which we carried them. Now that we were on our own in that cut, we had no idea how long we would be there, and the extra food could save our lives.

Those three brave men lay out there, their bodies seen by me only as outlines of elevated body-sized areas in the snow. The battery packs, which left almost no outline, took time to find. The impact of the mortar shell burst had flung them away from the bodies of the dedicated men who had carried them. That additional search time heightened the danger that, now that visibility was sharp and clear, an enemy who had sighted us operating there only the day before might now see me.

The enemy knew that somewhere in that panorama of thousands of acres, there was an artillery spotter and his radio operator that they must find. We knew it, too. We *must not* give away our location. Making a fire to keep us warm was out of the question. Even if we could find sticks of wood in that railroad cut (mostly stripped clean by the locals), lighting a fire with ice-saturated, and thus smoke-producing twigs, day or night, was too dangerous. We'd be dead meat.

In addition, there was now illumination everywhere. Some of the tanks we had set afire were still burning hours later. Their spilled gasoline had burned quickly, the heat often exploding their gas tanks and setting the slower-burning oils afire. Those tank treads literally floated in lubrication oil that, once ignited, burned and burned and burned. There were also occasional flare-ups from the smoldering village of Tillet lighting up the night. From time to time, Nazi mortars fired phosphorus shells skywards, throwing out intense light to look for all Americans but, most particularly us. Even without those man-made sources of light from the killing field, the now blizzard-free, star- and moon-lit skies alone could be our undoing.

Keeping warm by leaving our foxholes and walking around was not an option, either. When daylight came, lateral footprints in those drifts would have given us away to any of their scouting patrols or ground-hugging fighter planes (like the one that had strafed us in our trucks coming up from the Saar not long before).

Next daylight was Christmas.

Getting ready for our second day of King Tiger Tank hunting, I looked out over the fresh-fallen snow. Our kills were successively ever more westward, but no matter how many hundreds of yards away, the spotter and I could see the hulking ruins of each tank. We could also see from the blackened snow where each cluster of 155 mm shells we had caused to be fired "for location" had landed.

I climbed up the slope toward my one-man foxhole. Burning forever in my mind are the pictures of the landscapes that lay before me. After I slid into my daytime "home" on Christmas day of 1944, I realized that I was standing upright at the highest elevation in that whole sector of southeast Belgium. I took a good look all around me: the color of the winter sky at the eastern horizon was a brilliant winter red. Looking to the south, the horizon and the snow-covered hills that created it were tinted a bright orange. Standing out stark against them, the objects they contained all contributed to create a surrealistic painting far beyond the wildest imagination of a Salvador Dali.

Beautiful in pastel orange were some undulating waves of virgin-snow-covered hills. Others were not pristine, because they had been over-painted with blackened snow-outlined irregular patches where 155 mm shells had hit and spread death-dealing shrapnel in all directions. Also painted there, were burned-out or still fiery tank hulks and the other debris that our actions of the day before had caused. Helping to draw my eyes to each of these were zig-zagging tank-tread-patterned tracks in the snow, ending at the place where each tank's final lurch towards Bastogne had been terminated.

Roasted inside, or lying outside across their tanks' hulks, or lying grotesque in the snow nearby, were the remains of the fire-consumed bodies which had shortly before housed the souls of men — probably regular men who had had the misfortune of being entrapped by the warped ideologies of evil ones.

And Dali, at his most bizarre, was surely outdone here by Mars, the God of War, who had also employed warped-art as a trademark that jumped out at me when I turned to my north. Here, Mars had used broad ebon and reddish-brown brush strokes. The eye was directed to its centerpiece: the stark, blackened piles of brick and broken concrete which were all that remained of the war-torn, devastated village of Tillet.

At the end of our second day, we had killed another five Nazi King Tiger Tanks, and I slid down the slope at nighttime to our three-man foxhole. In our state of freezing and exhaustion, I changed my primary training objective to that of setting up and explaining rules to have us take turns keeping each other awake. While in the States, I had read in my Army manual about Arctic troops being cautioned against falling asleep in the bitter cold. I warned my two foxhole mates (teenagers like me) that we would have a staying-awake problem. The solution was to function as a team. I set it up.

I would pull the first two-hour shift and awaken the second shift man. At the end of his first two-hour shift he had to awaken his buddy. We had to take turns that way, with one of us always being awake, through each of the long nights we were to be together. The five kills we had made that second day were still burning, but being fewer and farther away than those of the first day, what little light they contributed (and that only to the top of our cut) was much less. Tillet's fires had died out and contributed nothing any more.

Any time it was my turn to stay awake, I would climb by now-available starlight back up the south side of the cut and awaken the lieutenant. That way he could get four hours sleep in between my visits. The time awake, we shared. He and I spent it in our respective nearby foxholes talking in a whisper about home. We both had radium dial watches that glowed in the dark. Then he'd go to sleep and I would return to my temporary home at the bottom of the cut. The system was that whoever's turn it was to stay awake would wear my radium dial watch, and each would pass it on to the next guy.

That corner of Belgium was bitter, bitter cold. Every breath we exhaled froze. Our five-day growths of beards were solid hoar frost above our mouth lines, and solid spittle below. Staying alive without that stay-awake plan in place, and adhered to, would have been impossible.

On December 26, the morning following the third night of our sub-zero deep-freeze, I was brought to consciousness by the glare of the sunlight on my closed eyelids. I shook myself awake, and elbowed the men on either side of me so I could reprimand whichever one was responsible for not keeping us awake.

They were both…frozen to death.

The man on my left and the man on my right were each facing me. Their ghastly rime-covered faces stared sightlessly at me. They haunt my dreams to this day.

I scrambled back up one last time on the snow-covered, solidly frozen slope to the lieutenant's foxhole hoarsely whispering, *"Your men are dead! Your men are dead!"*

When he did not answer, I feared what turned out to be true — the lieutenant too was dead. I turned him over to make sure.

I believe that I survived because I was positioned between the two others in the three-man foxhole. Their waning body heat must have just barely allowed me the extra margin of survival until the sun reflecting off of the brittle ice and snow awakened me.

The man who had failed us had to be the man wearing my watch, the poor soul. I took off my gloves and struggled with frozen fingers to loosen the freeze-stiffened strap, removed it from his wrist, and shoved it into my pocket to let the strap warm up to be supple once again. A watch was an important tool for a radio operator. Timing the arrival of scheduled incoming calls to or from HQ was often essential.

These three were not the first to die alongside of or near me, nor were they to be the last. I acknowledged their bravery and cursed the Nazi-driven, stupid, sheer waste of their promising futures, and then turned to the immediate business at hand. Before leaving the lieutenant I looked over the ledge of the foxhole that he had carved with his entrenching tool, and pocketed his K ration boxes in case I was further stranded and without food. Water was no problem…plenty of snow and ice to suck on. Then I slung his high-powered spotters' binoculars strap over my head, slid over to my radio, picked up my mike, snapped its toggle switch to the on position, and said into it: "Hello Victor Nan Victor, this is Nan Victor Charlie One. How do you read me? Over."

"We hear you 5 by 5," came booming back (great atmospherics that morning)[33]. This shattered the unearthly quiet of my frozen cut and its frozen occupants. I sharply twisted the volume dial down, but quick! Who knows what enemy patrols were out monitoring those now eerily silent hills which cradled a crushed village and 14 smashed King Tiger Tanks?

"Where the hell have you been?" the officer now hollered at me, but at a volume artificially dialed down to a whisper. "You were supposed to check in at daybreak!"

In a hoarse, shivering voice, I reported by names the fate of those three men (whose names soon joined the hundreds of names of men I had also briefly known and lost…names that would fade from memory in a matter of hours to days).

I carried the lieutenant's binoculars as a remembrance of him.

They knew the map coordinates of our location, of course. I had up-front transmitted them in code, for without them the gunners could not relate our position to that of our targets. With those coordinates they would direct their graves detail where to look for the six frozen

---

[33] 5 by 5 means loud and clear…5 out of 5 for loudness and 5 out of 5 for clarity.

bodies, and the things they had carried, when it was safe to do so. Victor Nan Victor told me they would call back in ten minutes by the clock with further instructions.

Suddenly finding myself with ten minutes of no responsibility, I started to cry uncontrollably, especially for the six men who had been so briefly, and so recently, my family. Such losses occurred often in other killing fields, but this was the first time my sorrow for my fellow soldiers came as the result of their freezing to death. My tears froze as they left my eyes.

Then my call letters came through and snapped me out of it.

"Hello Nan Victor Charlie One. Are your ears up?"

"This is Nan Victor Charlie One. I hear you 5 by 5."

They ordered me to switch frequencies back to my own Company L, and resume taking orders from them. It was natural for them to conclude that without the lieutenant, I was of no use to that artillery outfit. It never occurred to me to inform them of my ability to handle both jobs. Looking back, we had apparently run out of Nazi King Tigers to kill, anyway.

I was told to walk out the way I had come in (this implied moving along the railroad tracks in case the Nazis were listening), and to make it "quick, quick, quick!" My company really needed me and my radio. Not to mention that battalion headquarters was anxious to debrief me on what my "highest priority" new assignment had been all about. I had some explaining to do, of course. Privates don't just call their captains and ask if it's OK to move to another command without any questions as to why. I figured that battalion was in for a pleasant surprise: their decision to place Company L along that railroad track had accomplished something important after all.

They did not yet know that without the death of my three cut-and-fill Company L companions, I would not have been in the role of helping to destroy 14 King Tiger Tanks.

I slogged along the exposed fill where, three days before, I had gone out twice to retrieve the batteries. When I reached the prior cut, the men formerly there from Company L had already left, leaving single-file footprints. I stuck to their footprints as much as possible, to ease my way through the knee-high fluffy drifts. But below this most recent snow was earlier snow, which had become crusted-over with substantial ice. As expected, most of the footprints had rarely broken through this ice, but my extra 60 pounds of radio broke me through far more often than they had — even up to my thighs. Now, each time that happened, I had no one to help me out. I had to take off my radio, set it up onto the snowy surface, climb out, put it back on, and resume trudging. What probably took them a couple of hours, following each other's footprints to where the trucks had left us off, must have taken me over four. Not only did all three layers of snow-ice-snow slow me, but I also had an inefficient, limping gait from three days earlier, when shrapnel had hammered my rifle stock into my thigh.

Off to the side of a fill, I spotted a lone, burning farmhouse. The allure of its guaranteed heat was overwhelming. I detoured to it, and without a second thought, walked into what must have been the living room. My newly-acquired fear of freezing to death had overwhelmed the rational behavior of staying outside and warming up gradually, rather than risking my life by just plunging in. It turned out that walking into such heat was the worst thing you could do when body-frozen. I learned later that you're supposed to warm yourself up gradually. In that situation I should have first rubbed fire-warmed snow on my hands, face, feet, and ears — to bring temperatures up slowly.

The house did not look like a casualty of the fighting, as there was no impact damage. It was just a farmhouse in the last stages of being gutted by fire. The studs had tongues of flame licking up to the quietly burning rafters. A couple of those heavy cross-member beams fell while I was standing inside. I just didn't care. Just stood there. Warm. When I got warmed up, I walked back out again. Nonchalant. Just like that.

The moment I left that house and its rosy warmth, AGONY began to set in. The bitter, bitter cold, through its numbing effect, had acted as a painkiller. Nagging body pain was setting up residence that would take years to lessen. Returning "quick…quick…quick" was not so easy to do.

Then, too, I was alone with my God-centered thoughts and my new-found pain. As I struggled back along the route of my railroad tracks, I began to puzzle out what constituted aloneness. At a tender age, I was learning that it is not necessarily defined by any absence, or presence, of people around me. It's more a state of mind.

I was never in any place long enough to establish lasting wartime friendships. There are no Army outfit reunions in my life. No "Associations" of anybody who may have served in combat with me — primarily because most of those I knew were killed or evacuated, and only briefly known. I don't even know to this day what outfit I was temporarily in while taking out the King Tiger Tanks.

That stumbling walk back to L Company defined the parameters of aloneness that I have occasionally dwelt upon through the years. I am not given to depression, and being alone holds no terrors for me. But in those days when each frontline combat action was dominated by fear, loneliness assumed a whole new dimension — deepening my compassion for those who are alone into one which drives me still, though it is 66 years later.

When I finally made it back, I spilled all the details on King Tiger Tanks, but I had the feeling that the man who debriefed me could have cared less. After all, the artillery of some *other* outfit had claimed the kills by now, and my radio and I were needed elsewhere starting like right now! "Stop wasting my time with details," his body language said. Then I could imagine him saying, "What does a 19-year-old kid know about anything, anyway?!"

It was going to be slow, hard, stubborn fighting to take back what Hitler's breakthrough had won. Every man who could function at all was ordered back into combat, with no if's, and's, or but's. For obvious reasons, combat-experienced frontline radio operators were in especially short supply. The fact that my body now radiated extreme all-over pain with my every move made no difference. Back I went.

First it was to Luxembourg to re-fit — which provided some relief in startling ways.

Chapter 12: The Luxury of Luxembourg

The small nation of Luxembourg, squeezed between Belgium and Germany, felt keenly the curse of location, location, location in WWII. But at this moment, it and we had lucked out: Luxembourg was narrowly outside of the surge later known as The Battle of the Bulge, and the American forces that were dug in to defend it were still at full strength when we arrived to replace them for three days — complete with our just-rejoined-Company-L radio operator: me.

Image 28: Luxembourg

The incredibly bitter cold persisted, but there was no enemy on hand to bother us, and we operated in full (if unwarming) sunlight. What blessings!

In Luxembourg, we were defending a natural western flank border, the Moselle River, which when combined with an L-shaped foxhole-line, formed the front. The company we were to relieve had set its headquarters in another one of those bigwig Nazi estate manors overlooking a frozen river, a lot like the Saar estate must have looked before combat shelling. The Moselle had snow-covered slopes on both the US and Nazi banks. So far, no river crossing had been attempted here; the place was un-marred by any ground combat. The estate manor had been heavily damaged from the air, but its bomb-proof cellar was intact and still perfectly usable as our headquarters, so the captain moved us right in.

"Private Arnold," he said, "here's a map showing the foxhole locations that we need to cover as replacements. Take this man along with you to carry your radio." (My frozen back's now raw and dead skin prohibited me from carrying anything with straps.)

We only had one-fifth the manpower of the group we were replacing. So, the captain's instructions were to drop off one man into every fifth foxhole. Therefore, instead of the familiar terrain formula that dictated optimum distance between men on a front, each man could only guess the whereabouts of his nearest neighbors on either side of him, even in daytime. I plotted the location of each now-occupied foxhole. The sparsely-defended front line was a wide-open invitation for a repeat of the Bulge breakthrough of 12 days before. We could only hope that the Nazi war-machine had shot its wad this time.

Our inventory of combat necessities was severely compromised from heavy prior action. "Re-fitting" was a mild term hinting at the extreme danger we would be in, should we be challenged to fight before replenishing. For the three days of our re-fit, I carried a map where I marked an X for the location of each occupied foxhole, and the name of its occupant. It was snowing hard enough that our footprints disappeared quickly. We had a heck of a time re-finding each freshly-hidden foxhole. The shivering men who occupied them were replaced in unequal shifts, so that they could see where they were going in the short daylight hours of late December. Their off-duty times were spent in the fireplace-warmed rooms of the Chalet. The smoke was not a problem, because if the enemy had wanted to locate us, the big Chalet would have been a give-away, no matter what.

Things being quiet, our captain ordered his runners to explore the area not visible to the enemy from their side of the river. When these scouts looked over the edge of our river bank, they noticed a suspicious outcropping. Surprised by their own life-threatening curiosity, they moved down to explore it.

What they found was an ingeniously disguised entrance to a huge wine cellar!

They quickly and quietly grabbed a few bottles off the slanted aging-shelves, and came back to report their discovery to the Captain. It turned out that our First Lieutenant had been a liquor salesman in civilian life, so the Captain issued him a flashlight, as well as permission to sneak down to the wine cellar that night to take an eyeball inventory of the full extent of the cache. Meanwhile, we had a small amount of electric light inside the Chalet: the captain's idling jeep served as a generator that we cable-connected to a DC electric lantern. There being no fancy cork-pulling gadget in sight, someone opened a bottle by smashing its neck on the corner of a table, and the jagged-edged bottle was passed around. Because of its celebrated Moselle "nose", its non-foaming content, and its taste, it was unanimously declared to be fully-aged, really fine stuff.

The First Lieutenant found that the racks were organized by the vintage-stamped date, with the best of the lot nearest the door. Makes sense. The Captain formulated a plan. The first to benefit from the find would be his own Company L men who had put their lives on the line: the men I had just implanted into the foxholes.

The next morning, at daybreak, we started our wine distributing mission. The sub-zero cold continued, accompanied by wind strong enough to make for a virtual blizzard. Our snow prints of the day before were totally gone. I moved ahead with my two assistants behind me. They took turns lugging the radio, and dragging a big canvas duffel bag acting as its own sled for the wine bottles. Under these weather conditions, I led the men tentatively, using my compass and sketch-map of where each occupied foxhole was located. We were like a ship in a full gale…almost no visibility. Though there was only one wine trip to the foxholes that day, we made several trips to the men, shuttling precious thermos canteens of hot soup. This they had to drink quickly, because despite the thermos insulation, the surrounding cold immediately reduced hot to warm… and warm to frozen. Each of the night shift troops put the thermos into his pants to preserve its warmth as far into the night as possible. As long as the driving wind blew, neither of my men could turn back on his own. No-man's-land is a terrible place to get lost.

Because of our two-shifts-a-day scenario, our foxhole strength was only 25 men, widely scattered over a front that could have used 125. All along, the wine-toting man was automatically signaling ahead in the blizzard by the clinking of the bottles as he dragged his duffel load forward. We arrived at each foxhole with our precious gift, and I followed the captain's orders: deliver each man one-and-only-one bottle, relaying the captain's admonition that it would have to be carefully nursed through the next two days and nights of re-fitting. Anyone getting drunk would be a danger to the others, and would not be issued a next go-round's bottle.

Good plan. Smart man. The plan worked.

Our Moselle wine cellar was loaded with the very best quality stuff but not one man got tipsy. After all, there was too much at stake, and everyone knew it. Once we had put some aside for the Company L fighting men, the captain radio'd General Patton's headquarters to notify them of our find. A major from Old Blood and Guts' Quartermaster Corps came and took over the distribution of the goods from the Wine Cellar. A requisitioning system, complete with paperwork, was established. Officers' command cars came and went to various units' headquarters, with each of their apportionments on board.

Officers being officers, I doubt if any wine trickled down to enlisted men levels — except for the three days when Company L controlled the wellhead. During that time, our ex-liquor-salesman Lieutenant held court in the Great Room of the Chalet, teaching us all, enlisted men and officers alike, a thing or two about his trade. He explained that if you uncorked the bottle and no bubbles welled up, the aging was just right.

As it turns out, an estimated fifty *thousand* bottles lay in the huge cave under the ground at that place. Our HQ guys could afford to be picky. They would remove the cork, and if bubbles emerged, they would hurl that bottle into the giant main room's fireplace, creating a soul-satisfying shower of broken glass, accompanied by its liquid bubbly sliding into the grated ashes, and down the drain. They soon tired of cork-removing, and speeded things up by smashing the neck of each bottle against the side of the fireplace. No one worried about the jagged edges of glass as they drank the bubble-less ones — least of all me, the teetotaler.

If this seems wasteful to you now, remember that the source of all this wealth was the looting of local French and Belgian wineries by this Chalet's Nazi owner, who had employed slave labor to build his storage and aging facilities — slaves long since gassed and incinerated in the so-called concentration camps nearby.

By our last sustenance run to the foxholes, the weak meteorological front had just moved through, and the strong winds were finally subsiding. We were following our dim footprints through the settling snow, when, about half way back to the Chalet, we were astounded to see scores of boot-print trails crossing our path from the enemy's side…and new within the last hour. We were badly outnumbered to say the least.

We threw ourselves to the ground.

Chapter 13: Who the Hell Are You?

After a pause, and staying on our bellies, we started edging our way back to the Chalet via the next of our foxhole positions, fully expecting to see our man lying there with his throat cut. With this many enemy, there was no way he had survived — and we had heard no gunshots.

But there he was, standing tall in his foxhole, giving us a friendly wave. I figured that an enemy sniper already had him in his sights, and we were being led into a trap. Do I dare to break the silence of that snowy scene, and give away our position by calling in our dilemma to the Captain? What could he do about it anyway? All of his man-power, even down to the battalion's cooks and bakers, were already with us. Surely we have bought the farm… we are all dead men.

Then, to our utter amazement, from out of the snowy patch of woods behind his foxhole came dozens of white-clad enemy infantrymen, all weaponless, with arms held over their heads in the universal sign of surrender.

"Hande de hoch!" (hands up!) we foolishly shouted in our confused mix of fear and relief. (It was certainly obvious that their hands were already up.) Our surprised man in the foxhole trained his M1 Garand in the general direction of the group and shouted, "You are my prisoner!" Then he turned to me as the head of our returning wine-carriers and inquired, "What will I do with them?"

In all of my 19 years on this earth, I had never encountered anything like this before. I called the Captain and explained the situation.

"First, motion them to lower their arms," he said. (Obviously, none of them was about to go for weapons that they weren't carrying.) Then he added, "If any of them speaks English, ask him who they are."

I did, and one did.

"He claims that they are Luxembourgers who were impressed into the German army when the Nazis overran their country in 1940.

"They were wearing Nazi uniforms when the Americans started counter-attacking yesterday, and while the Nazis were busy fighting back, these men simply shot their Nazi officers and walked out, heading in the general direction of here — when they finally stumbled upon this American in his foxhole and surrendered to him."

Then the Captain asked through his jeep-mounted radio, "Where do the map coordinates of the foxhole say you are?" When I radioed back, he said, "OK. Leave your guy in his foxhole, and I'll send one of our bakers with a loaded rifle to escort the prisoners to the road, which is only 100 yards away. My jeep driver will be waiting for you there. Tell the baker to hand his rifle to the jeep driver, and man the jeep's machine gun. Have him aim at the center of the bunch, and in that way he and the driver will progress down the road, herding them back to the Chalet where we'll take over. I'll get Division MP's to take them as prisoners of war, and they'll probably be interned in a camp in the USA. Meanwhile, I'll get some guys here to start stringing a barbed wire enclosure inside this Chalet to hold them for now. When my jeep gets back with my radio, I'll contact the MP's.

"And by the way, Private Arnold, good work. If you run across any more surrendering troops on your way back, we'll handle them the same way." We actually did run across another bunch trying to surrender from the rear. They walked right through our line, and then milled around, looking for someone to surrender to!

After a few days, our re-fitting was complete. I got a brand new radio, and a spare one to draw on. After we got enough fresh-off-the-boat replacement teenager GI's to build us up to normal company strength, we headed back into the thick of the battle in Belgium. When the next outfit came in for re-fitting, I led them to the line of foxholes we had vacated, and handed my map to the guy in charge.

Our luxurious Luxembourg winter three-day vacation was over — even though my excruciating pain was not.

Chapter 14: Back to the Front

We set out to gain back our lost ground in the snow and cold, back to the original front before The Bulge started. The Nazis gave ground grudgingly.

I was horribly frozen. Every day of that fight back to the German border was accomplished in a nightmare of pain. From my commanding officers' points of view, the fact that I was severely ice-burned played a distant second to my communications training. I was a self-propelled brain. Even with frozen feet and fingers and nose and ears, I was a part of the counter-attack over the snow, over the hills, pushing again eastward toward the German border till mid-January. Because my deep-freeze burned skin could be intolerably painful to touch, my 60-pound radio now always had to be carried by someone else. My field pack and rifle were too much for my skin; others were designated to carry them for me. Even the strap of the binoculars caused intolerable chest and shoulder pain. I had to give up carrying them in remembrance of the FO lieutenant who had adopted me for killing the King Tiger Tanks. In my frozen state, I just barely managed the small weight of the mike-and-earphone headset that was attached by a long wire to the radio. Forget the helmet...too heavy. In this unique manner I trudged back nearly to the German border, through ice and snow, with my Company L outfit. Two burly privates were assigned the job of keeping me alive and moving. One died protecting me on January 8th, and was replaced by another.

Whenever we were stopped by hard-fighting, or the unforgiving miserable weather, I had to be eased either into a ditch, onto a snow-covered fallen tree, or three times where there were no trees, onto a nearby, frozen Nazi soldier's body. We refused to sit on American bodies, although there were plenty of them around awaiting pickup when it would be safe for the burial detail to operate in the area. When it was time to move on, I had to be assisted back to my feet.

In exchange for others having to carrying my equipment, I did what only I was qualified to do: work that radio as a pro for Company L. And I had the military map reading skills which my new commander learned he could lean on with confidence. And despite my lousy grade of 64 in military school foreign language, by now, I could also interpret French.

All around us there were homeless refugees of several nationalities living in war-torn basements of what were once homes. Many were French, or French-speaking Belgians, who had been pressed into Nazi slave labor underground factories just over the German border. As a result of our new tentative post-Bulge border crossings, they were recently freed — and anxious to help us defeat their former captors. Through my halting French-English translations, they gave us vital information on the enemy troops waiting for us as we advanced.

Many of these refugees survived by eating — voraciously — the leftover food we dumped into our garbage pits. Having seen what their starving hunger really looks like, I've never since put anything on my plate that I cannot eat. In a mess hall, the standard is pretty much like what you see in the movies, with the server slopping a huge portion of food onto the soldiers' plates. Now, when having the luxury of being in a mess line, I began to say, "No, no. Just give me half of that," or whatever I thought I could eat without wasting. I wasn't the only one who developed this sensitivity in the War; I heard others around me asking for less, too — and for the same reason.

When we were lucky enough to come upon a fire to warm ourselves by, I could not participate. At this point, I *needed* the bitter cold as much as I *hated* it. Its numbing effect was the only thing that made the pain of my frozen body parts bearable. How cold was it? Spit froze before hitting the ground. All vehicles had to be started up every 30 minutes, or, anti-freeze and all, they became useless.

I myself was to become useless as a result of the bitter cold. I contracted pneumonia, and was finally evacuated to a field hospital. (Company L went on, and made it to the German border seven days later.)

I waved a not-in-the-least-bit-fond good-bye to my lousy radio. I was too sick to talk to anybody. My Captain was kind enough to tell me that I would be missed, and he wished me a quick recovery. He had already appointed the sharper of my two current ARO's to take over until he lucked out once again and got another guy with radio school training.

In my condition, I couldn't have cared less. I was one sick, worn out, teenaged, American GI Joe.

Image 29: Field Hospital Somewhere in Normandy – June / July 1944

The poor guys who followed me would have to continue to face the most experienced army the world had ever seen: Hitler's fighting machine, battling desperately now on its own snow-and-ice-clad western borders. There were tough days and weeks and months yet to go, and it was highly likely that I would soon be back in the thick of it, if I lived long enough.

When I had pneumonia as a child, it required both medicine and weeks of bed-rest. But this time, the doctors and nurses introduced something new into my cough-wracked body. They gave me shots of "penny-cillin". Never heard of it before. The doctors injected it into me in a pyramidal-tent field hospital.

This miracle drug was, of course, penicillin. It knocked out those pneumonia bugs just like that! There I was in the hospital and the penicillin had worked and the doctor said, "Hey, Private Arnold, here's your papers. We're sending you back to your outfit."

"Wait a minute — I'm *frozen!*"

"What do you mean, 'frozen'?"

"A few days ago, on the front line. Please just take a look." I told him that the six men who had been with me had died from deep-freezing. (I am not talking frostbite here. I am talking frozen *solid*.)

"Oh. my God," he said. "All over your body…the equivalent of third degree burns." He closely examined my hands, feet, and ears…the body extremities farthest from the warming blood of the heart.

"Why didn't you tell me in the first place?"

"I did. Nobody was listening."

"Well, we're listening now. We're going to sedate you and send you to a hospital with a special ward to treat you."

The last thing I remember is the jab of the needle…

Chapter 15: Frozen Nearly Unto Death

I awoke on a cot, in a long hallway of cots, with men in various stages of awareness lined up on both sides. When I finally came completely to my senses, I noticed a black box on my chest. I reached for it, and looked at it, turning it over in my hands. It said "Purple Heart" on the outside.

Image 30: The Purple Heart

I was now a battle-scarred teenaged veteran of bitter combat in World War II. As I looked down the row of cots on either side of me, I noticed that some of those other men had the Purple Heart box on their chests, but most of the boxes had slipped off and fallen on the floor as the men had stirred in their sleep. I had evidently slept like a rock, because my box was undisturbed. Unfortunately, as I became more and more awake, I also became more and more aware of pain from my freeze-burns. The medics moved me to a large ward with tents made out of sheets over each of the beds. Some of these sheets were rolled back and the beds were empty. They carefully picked me up and laid me onto one of the beds.

I noticed that everybody in the room was male and soon found out why. The attendants stripped me naked and elevated various points of my body to put padded blocks under them:

my heels, thighs, buttocks, waist, shoulders, elbows, wrists, and head. This was to minimize the points where my body contacted the bedding. They gave me another shot to reduce the pain.

When I awoke again there were no empty beds, and soon after, a male nurse pulled back the sheets and started to peel dead skin from my ears, nose, toes, and fingers. Every morning a male nurse would come in to strip from my naked body any skin that had become more easily removable since the day before. As each part was stripped, it revealed the bright red re-growth underneath.

After nearly three months of this routine, the pressure-point blocks, and the straps that had held me rigidly in place on them, were removed. That skin, too, was now free to heal. Once most of the new skin's color turned to normal, life at the end of the hospitalization was at last comfy. They let me get up and walk around. At last, I was free to roam the hospital and explore for pastimes. My hospital was a converted school for girls in St. Cloud[34], just outside of Paris.

I discovered checkers and other games (video games were another whole generation away). But the primary attraction for everyone was the motion picture theatre, which they had set up in the school's cafeteria. The hospital bulletin boards posted the coming attractions from Hollywood, and since we longed for sights of home, we saw every picture over and over, until the next one arrived. One day, I noticed that the new attraction was Benny Goodman's "Music in Wartime". Well, I was at the Hotel New Yorker the night it was filmed! That was the night the maître d' placed my gorgeous date and me right on the stage at the curve of the piano. So once the movie's run started, I went to every showing — stopping only for dinnertime and bathroom breaks. I hollered out "Oh my gosh! That's me right there at the table on the stage!" And all the teenaged male soldiers watching with me never failed to holler back, "The hell with you…who's the beautiful broad you're with?!" We went through the same routine over and over, and I loved every minute of it.

Not long before discharge, I had a visitor. It was Rabbi Erwin Hyman, of the conservative temple in Syracuse. Those of you who know about Judaism know there are three most common branches: reform (most modernized), conservative (middle of the road), and orthodox (most traditional). My family belonged to the reform Temple in town, and Rabbi Hyman was

---

[34] The French pronunciation is "SAn- cloo".

from the conservative Temple. But the Jewish community in a city the size of Syracuse was not very large and most everybody knew everybody else. In fact, our two groups often did things together, so we knew each other pretty well. When the Rabbi walked into my ward, we flung our arms around each other and settled in for a little schmoozing[35] about the good old days in Syracuse before the war. It turns out that this Rabbi from my home town was the chief of Jewish Chaplains for all forces under General Eisenhower's command. His job was to visit Jewish casualties throughout the whole European Theatre of war.

He could see that, under the circumstances, I was doing well. The constant, spontaneous pain was gone. (I did not yet realize that I would still be unable to stand the straps of anything on my shoulders.) He had arranged for me to take a day's leave to see the sights of Paris under his supervision. He told me that I would be picked up by his command vehicle one morning soon.

When that day came, I was all dressed up in my Army best and went out to the front gate, and there awaited a limousine! Not a command vehicle at all, but a good old fashioned limo, with fender flags boasting that it carried a Major. A uniformed driver was standing by the door of the car.

"Private Arnold, I am your personal driver for the day."

You can imagine how flattered I was. He took me for a tour of Paris, including a very fine restaurant (all expenses paid), and then he drove me to the afternoon's entertainment: the world famous Folies Bergere. I got out of the car to see a whole line of GI's waiting to get admission tickets. But my driver deposited me at the head of the line, saluted me, and told me he would pick me up when the show was over. Everybody in the long line snapped to attention because they expected a major to emerge; they couldn't have known that the entire limo was only for little old Private me! By that time, they had already flashed the salute, and I saluted them back. I was, in every sense of the word for that moment in time, a VIP.

I went right in and took my seat in a beautiful theatre. The appointments were sensational. Clowns warmed up the audience, speaking in both French and English in deference to the many soldiers present. We sang songs and everything was just as beautiful as could be.

---

[35] In this context, the Yiddish word *schmoozing* means enjoyable conversation and reminiscing. No English word captures it quite as well.

When the show started, the chorus line had my total attention, because every one of those gorgeous girls was *topless*, and the bobbing and swaying of their breasts had us all immediately falling in love with the whole bunch of them.

Image 31: Advertising Poster for Follies Bergère

I wondered…does the Rabbi know where he sent me for entertainment?! I was too embarrassed ever to ask him, but I'll say this: I was entertained!

Finally after three months, I was discharged from the hospital on April 10, 1945. I would itch, and itch, and itch for the rest of my life, but that was a small trade-off for being alive. I was snapped awake at 0500 by a pre-recorded bugle call blaring through the radio speakers in our ward. As the skies began to lighten, a new chapter of my Army life began. Over my tender new skin, with my long-john underwear and winter uniform shirt as padding to protect my tender bod, I donned my factory-new field pack and was ready for wherever next the gods of war were about to take me.

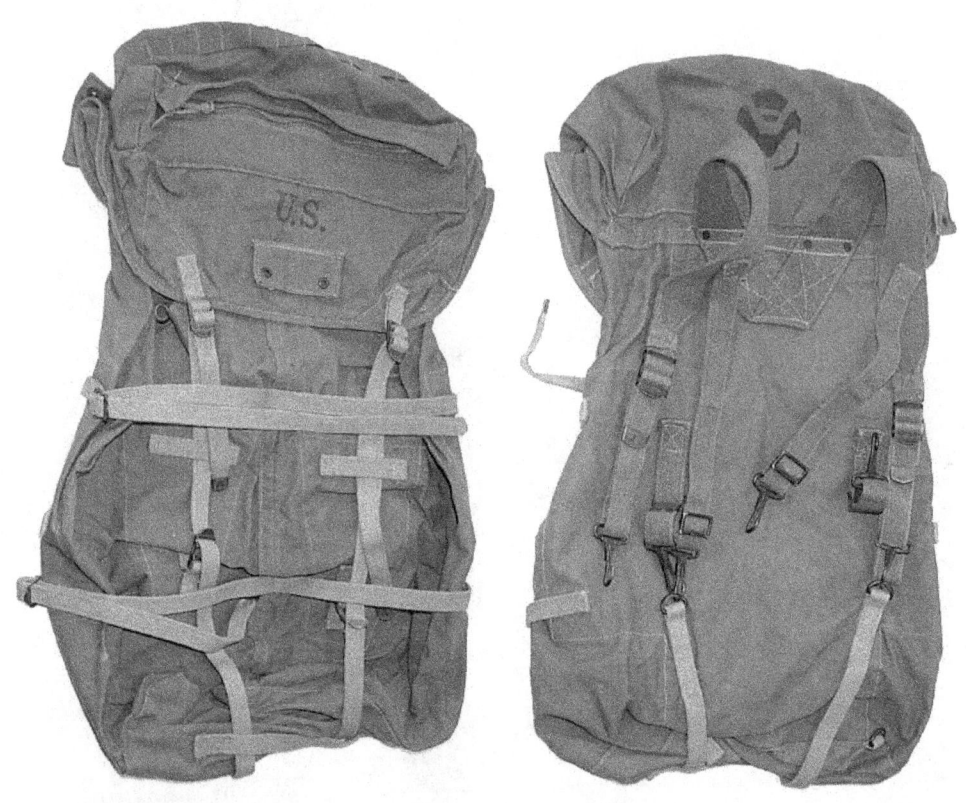

Image 32: WWII M1943 Field Pack

Check-out time was after 1100 hours, because priority clerical time was devoted to processing the endless stream of incoming wounded arriving the night before.

As instructed, I presented myself to the Records Section. They handed me a copy of my updated personnel file and asked me to check it for errors. It was my first time seeing that the Purple Heart Medal was official. That was also the day that I was able to put two and two together: by now I had repeatedly heard about The Battle of the Bulge, but till that day I never realized that when the news radio in my ward was talking about *that* battle, it was talking about *my* battle. I thought again about the six men who had frozen to death getting me to where we had destroyed those 14 huge Nazi tanks.

I noticed that the paperwork showed me in some heavy-artillery battalion for the three days when I stumbled into the opportunity to help dispose of the King Tigers, but it never occurred to me to memorize the name on those papers citing which artillery outfit I was so briefly in. All I remember is that the papers totally omitted my switching back to Infantry Company L for the next thirty days, before falling to pneumonia. At the time, I figured what's thirty days compared to my grand total of 19 years? They weren't about to quibble with little ol' Private Arnold about such a detail, so I signed off, and they date-stamped everything. They wished me luck and waved me down the hall to The Transportation Office for further instructions.

Although further hospitalization was unnecessary, I was, of course, far from "all better". Before my hospitalization, my ice-burned skin was too raw to support the strap of a binoculars. At the time of hospital discharge, my skin was exquisitely painful for a different reason: it was tender from being so new. Whatever the weather, *any* pressure was unbearable. More rubber-stamping of my copy of the personnel file, including the best one of all: I was now officially classified as Walking Wounded. With that title in my files, they could no longer send me back to the front lines.

After I ate, the re-assignment officials wished me good luck. I briskly walked out into the glorious, peaceful mid-day sunshine, and found my way past several of the former girls-school's classroom entrances to the one serving as waiting area for transportation.

I was a different guy from the weather-destroyed mess I was when I woke up in that hospital, just three months before. Now, not assigned to anybody, I temporarily stashed my new file in the newly-issued GI field pack. I had already mailed my Purple Heart Medal home to my sweetheart to keep for me.

I was issued a few pairs of socks, and a Dopp-kit of toilet articles including a small shaving mirror and razor. I would be given K rations when I reached my new outfit, whatever and wherever it was to be.

They strapped a rolled up summer-weight sleeping bag to my field pack, and after three months of re-growing my skin, I was back in the business at hand: helping to make things miserable for the Nazis.

Chapter 16: Paris in the Springtime

My next destination: the closest Army Replacement Depot. Replacement depots are not necessarily what they sound like to those unfamiliar with the military: they had nothing to do with the replacement of broken goods and supplies. Their function was to serve as staging hubs for the deployment, or redeployment, of troops where they were needed most. To put it bluntly, they had nothing to do with replacing broken *parts*. Their purpose was to deal with the replacement of broken *men*.

My transport driver was parked at the curb with a green 4x4[36] bearing a handwritten sign that read, "Replacement Depot". Two men were leaning against the hood, already waiting for me so we could all leave. They were GI Joes of maybe 18 or 19 like I was, and each carried an M-1 Rifle. As a communications man (which my file still showed), I had just been issued the shorter, three-pound lighter version: the M-1 Carbine. It was just like the one whose cedar-wood stock had saved my thigh, and therefore my life, by deflecting a chunk of deadly shrapnel three months before.

Compared to us, our thirty-something-year-old driver was middle-aged. We introduced each other all around, tossed a coin to see who would win the honor of sitting alongside the driver for the first leg of what he said would be a long ride, and the other two of us made ourselves comfortable on the truck bed's sideways-facing slab seats. I didn't mind. It was April 10, 1945, and the April in Paris sunny weather was bringing May flowers right on schedule. No one ever appreciated springtime more than I did on that day. Flowers were blooming, people whose villages had been recently liberated were eating regularly and smiling once again, and their grasses and crops were doing nicely, thank you. The foliage was beginning to hide the scars and wounds of last year's battles, prayerfully until the end of time.

We did another coin-flip to determine the order of front-seat rotation for the rest of the trip. We traveled at incredible vehicle speeds, via an unheard-of miracle of modern transportation: the Autobahn. Its ability to quickly deliver Nazi troops of Hitler's 3rd Reich from one battleground to another during Hitler's conquest of Europe was an extremely important weapon of war, now working for our side. This section of it was now in Allied hands, and we marveled

---

[36] 4x4 means 4 wheels with 4-wheel drive. 6x6 means double back wheels with all 6 serving as drive wheels.

at it. We were speeding along the four-lane divided highway. German Autobahns were the only such highways in the world. No one could deploy troops and their heavy weaponry between major population centers faster than the Nazis. General Eisenhower was now himself in direct command of the Allied-liberated part of that European network, and eight years later as President, inspired by the Nazi ingenuity seen then, he proposed the American Interstate Highways System that now bears his name.

When it was my turn to sit in the front passenger side of the single full-width seat, I watched the speedometer. The needle climbed to the stop-pin at 70 miles per hour, but my personal seat-of-the-pants built-in speedometer guessed that we continued to move up about another 10 mph past the dashboard gauge for almost the whole trip. Total blackout made travel at night an invitation to destruction from more than air attacks: in their retreat, the Nazis had lavishly used concentration camp slave labor to embed land-mines in their high-speed roads. In the daytime, any breaks in the cement were visible and steered around; but they were not visible in a total blackout. Travel was in daytime only.

In about three or four places along the way, we came to Autobahn bridges that had been blown-out by the retreating Nazis, or bombed-out by Allied air forces. At these sites we had to carefully wend our way down S-curving roads to river-level, and drive across assembled-on-the-site steel truss bridges floated on pontoons, and then 'S' on up the other side. These imported-from-the-USA bridges had been put together by Allied Army engineer outfits.

We rode until early dusk found us arriving just in time for blackout at our driver's target for that day: a 3,000-unit US pyramidal-tent city, pitched near the runways of Frankfurt am Main[37] (Germany's largest airfield in WWII).

On arrival at the Frankfurt Tent City, our driver used his truck-mounted radio to check in with whichever outfit kept tabs on him each time he passed through. One of the key functions of a tent city was to make sure that transients coming through were where they were supposed to be and not just on a sight-seeing lark, wandering aimlessly on their own in "borrowed" Army vehicles. They fed us at the main mess on arrival, and we went right to sleep.

I didn't know it yet, but we were about to be on the road to a teenager's hell.

---

[37] Pronounced "am-MINE".

Chapter 17: The Road to Hell

In April of 1945, daylight was starting to show around 0500 ETO-time[38]. We were rousted out of our borrowed cots, each given a breakfast pack and hot coffee, while our driver signed us out, and we piled back into the 4x4 to finish out the remaining miles of our journey. I heard him connecting again through the Tent City switchboard, and thence onto a land-line, to whomever was in charge of wherever it was we were going. As a frontline communications man, I knew all about radio-to-telephone protocol.

Our driver was assigned to that one Replacement Depot full time, shuttling healed men to it from the St. Cloud hospital, and (since his vehicle was not an ambulance) returning empty. As the front lines moved a little deeper into Germany, his Replacement Depot (or "Repple Depple" as we referred to it) also moved forward, maybe once a week at that stage in the war. So, within his three-times-a-week schedule, his eastward destination from one week to the next did not advance very far. He thus knew the way, only having to check out the last few kilometers on each trip to see if his Repple Depple had moved forward with our advancing Army.

For this final leg of our journey to the nearest Replacement Depot, there was no Autobahn. That meant it would take about three-and-a-half hours. In those days, the Spring-softening ground made for unpredictable roads. But someone had figured out how to attach bulldozer-shaped blades to tanks, jerry-rigging them to serve as road graders. With a little luck, our 4x4 could make good time. As we got closer to our Repple Depple, we saw that those 'dozers had done a good job, and recently. There were signs of fresh debris from recent tank battles and air strikes. Oftentimes Nazi tanks, whose treads swam in oil, would burn for a day or two after being hit by incendiaries, accidently creating an effective road block. But none of that immoveable debris blocked the road we were on.

Finally, later that morning we arrived at our Repple Depple destination. Having never seen a Replacement Depot before, I was prepared for anything from a small installation to a sprawling one, where perhaps hundreds of replacements coming in off a boat from The States could be processed and assigned and moved on to battle grounds in very short order. As it turns

---

[38] ETO stands for "European Theatre of Operations", meaning local time in Europe.

out, ours was as rudimentary as could be. It consisted of a damaged cement-block hut bearing a temporary thatched roof, and sitting in a dismal, dirt parking lot. Its only other features were a telephone land-line snaking along the roadside and into the hut's front door; plus a makeshift extension for the jeep antenna, made by running a wire from its tip on up a tall tree. We had often climbed trees trailing antenna-wire in combat, knowing only too well that if a Nazi sharp-shooting sniper spotted us, we were goners. The two of my 12 ARO's who had already earned Purple Heart Medals that way were certified heroes. As the current front line was at least several kilometers away, this particular climb had been done in safety. The parked jeep bore a sign saying "Replacement Depot # So-and-So", followed by a buck-sergeant's rank symbol.

Our pick-up truck driver drove as close as possible to the one door. As he braked to a stop, the hut's door flew open, and an excited buck sergeant, bearing a clipboard holding a yellow legal-pad, dashed out, flung the driver's door open, told him not to move, and held up his clipboard. We two truck-bed men stood up to see for ourselves. The pad held a rudely sketched line-art map with the road we had come in on shown running on past the Repple Depple hut in a generally north direction. It came to a dead stop about five kilometers (three miles) north of us, at what was evidently a German twin-village whose compound name he had hand-printed at the top of his quick-sketch map.

I, for one, was not happy about being amidst the recent smoking debris near this hut. It indicated that we were close to the present front lines. We were now being told to move even three miles *closer*. I said to the sergeant, "Hey wait, we're Walking Wounded. What are we doing looking at recent combat ruins, in an obvious war zone that Walking Wounded soldiers are not supposed to be fighting in?"

He was not interested in any of that nonsense. He wasn't listening. The other man in the back with me said something like: "Just let us get down from this truck and take a leak, and stretch our legs. We've been on the road since crossing into Germany."

"Don't you dare move off that truck!" our Repple Depple guy shouted. "This clipboard page (which he then tore off and shoved at the driver) is what I wrote down, just as it was described to me over the radio. Direct orders from the top… from *General George S. Patton himself!* It was him! He said to me, 'Those three you say you got coming…I want them here AT ONCE!' So if you guys have to piss or shit, do it in your pants! Patton said that you were to be there in FIVE minutes from the time you hit here. And with Patton, 'Five' minutes means THREE! Your road will end at a huge gate. A master sergeant will be standing right there. He will own your asses for as long as he needs you. Then I get you back for re-assignment. Leave your papers with me."

The driver restarted the engine, handed over our files, and backed around to head up the road sketched on the map. The names the buck sergeant had phonetically scrawled in big letters across the top were "Buke and Vald", obviously twin communities of which none of us had ever heard. We bounced over what was now a two-lane black-top road, which had easily broken up into chunks under the pounding of tanks and other army vehicles, and of course disintegrated where an occasional artillery shell had created a sizeable hole. There was the usual collateral junk connected with very recent combat, including all kinds of motor-driven vehicles, plus even some pitiful horse-drawn wagons which had once contained dislocated families and their precious possessions. Once in a while, there were a couple of civilian bodies, or a stripped-of-valuables Nazi soldier who, like the now-dead horses still attached to their traces, had given his all — random bombs and bullets do not discriminate according to the righteousness of the causes they serve. Given our driver's response to General Patton's personal orders, each passing moment that our pick-up truck remained upright was a renewed blessing. I could just visualize us hitting a chunk of debris, bouncing ass-over-teacups down the road, and sending us back to the hospital or worse. The distance to the gated road's end turned out to be about five kilometers, as advertised.

Because I had been in frontline combat situations where putrefying enemy bodies had not been retrieved for days, I knew that unmistakable smell of decay. In The Bulge, Army units called Burial Details had all they could handle finding America's fallen men, temporarily burying them, and carefully plotting the sites on maps for others to later find and properly inter. The Nazi dead were not their responsibility. But all of that was mild, compared to what we began to smell in the last mile of approach to The Gate on that April day. It was that same smell of death, but multiplied…over…and over…and over…as we drew nearer.

As we approached the fancy Gate straight ahead, obviously at the dead-end of our road, our nostrils were assailed by the most unholy stench — worse than could ever have been imagined.

I'll never know if the other three guys held their piss and shit, but in spite of my valiant efforts trying to hold mine in, I was about to lose it.

Note to the Reader Before Entering Buchenwald

To the reader —

Before I take you into Buchenwald, I must tell you what to expect; why, after all these years, I am publishing my experiences there as a 19-year-old soldier; and finally, I must also express my hope for what you will do as a result of my taking you inside The Gate.

<u>What to expect from Buchenwald</u>: The 28 hours of my life there are forever burned into my memory. All five senses were attacked: *sight*, by the piles of defiled dead bodies; *smell*, by the stench of decay, vomit, feces, and piss; *taste*, by that of my own bile and vomit; *touch*, by the slime covering the living and the dead alike; and *sound*, by the moans, cries, and sobs of grief…everywhere…everywhere…everywhere.

Up till my hospitalization, my exposure to extreme danger had been limited mostly to my body. But Buchenwald…Buchenwald threatened my mind. To give you an idea of the relative magnitudes involved, before approaching The Gate, my cumulative experience involved: witnessing the death of every man I had trained with for the past nine months all within a few hours of my first day on the front line; learning to voluntarily piss and shit in my pants in order to stay alive in ice-water-filled foxholes; watching all three others of my railroad expedition die from a mortar shell; awakening to see the frozen-to-death face portraits of all three others from my impromptu FO team; learning that when you're freezing to death, the intense heat that you crave so much can only hurt you more; that the world can be so upside down that you have to resolve to kill perfect strangers; that there is literally such a thing as being frozen stiff, and that in such a state, it is possible to be grateful for an enemy's dead body to sit on; that being stricken by a deadly pneumonia can *save* your life as easily as take it; that you can lose the majority of your skin and survive — in exchange for long-lasting pain; and finally, that sometimes, pissing and shitting your pants is not your choice to make. Let's say that the emotional impact of all that added together rates a 50 on some psychological scale of 1-100. On that same scale, and all by itself, Buchenwald would be a 100. No wonder its legacy has been undiminished nightmares throughout my two-thirds of a century since.

<u>Why I am finally publishing my experiences there as a 19-year-old soldier</u>: Against all odds for a World War II frontline combat radio operator, I was allowed to live. No matter how painful for me to revisit, I feel an obligation to pass along what I know. Not *every* lesson needs to be re-learned by humanity the hard way. Some lessons we are obligated to teach from one generation to the next, and to do so with fervor — even at the expense of opening the storyteller's old wounds. I am now 86, and active and lucid, but no one lives forever. I must pass along these horrible things as a contribution to humankind's getting past its endless cycle of hatred, injury, and retribution.

<u>My hope for what you will do as a result of my taking you inside The Gate</u>: The next few chapters necessarily describe horrific events, and contain deeply disturbing images. Yet, the point is not to sensationalize. It is to enlist. Here's the secret: the true mark of humanity's potential is not how good our memories are for who wronged whom, but looking forward to see how humanity cares for its weakest members everywhere[39].

Meanwhile, in honor of the scores of people who died right next to me, and the millions of others whose deaths I never saw, please do not find in this book any support for the hatred of any living people.

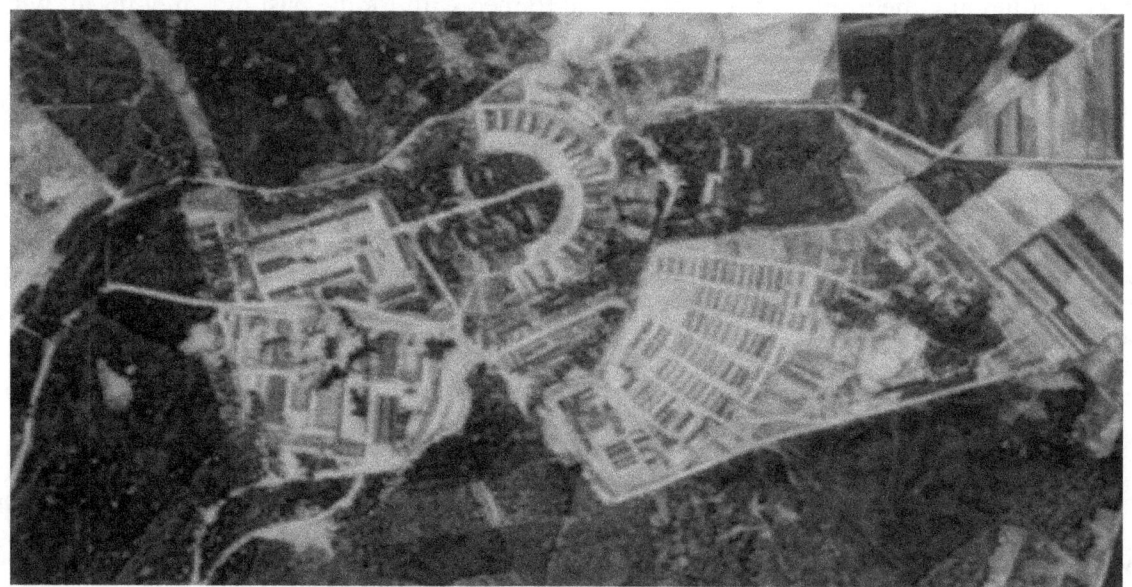

Image 33: Aerial View of Buchenwald 1945

---

[39] There are many precedents for this spirit, going back at least as far as the Old Testament (*i.e.* the Jews' Torah), which enjoins those who would listen to give special care to widows, orphans, strangers, the fatherless, the poor, the hungry, and the sick.

Chapter 18: The Master Sergeant, and The Gates of Buchenwald

Image 34: Outside the Gates of Buchenwald

April 11, 1945.

By the time our driver braked to a stop at that Gate, the stench had gone from insidious to absolutely overpowering. Visitors to Holocaust museums see pictures and read captions, but they can never smell the atrocious, foul odors. My nightmares always start with those foul odors, somehow recreated by the cells of my brain. Medical experts like my nephew-in-law, say the smell-factor in cases like mine is quite common, and that those who suffer from such nightmares attach to it an odor from their real life's experience, which they then label as such. Mine I label "The Stench of the Building of Pure Horror".

Beyond what we smelled was what we saw. Several meters inside that fancy Gate was the most nightmarish of views that could ever have been conjured up by even the most depraved of horror story writers: grotesque heaps of human corpses piled-up on top of one another as if into so many cords of firewood.

The two of us standing in the back of the truck began throwing up — first, all over the pick-up bed, and then over the sides. Stomachs out of control, we splashed some of that vomit over ourselves. We puked, and puked, and puked until there was no more left to throw up, and then we continued to dry heave for some minutes more. Shortly after the stench had stricken *us*, the cab-seated men also began throwing-up, flinging themselves out through their respective doors.

The Master Sergeant, an "old man" of about 40 that we were to report to, was standing outside of the huge Gateway that marked the end of our map road at "The Twin Villages of Buke and Vald". He was obviously talking to International Red Cross personnel, as indicated by their armbands. The Third Army Headquarters had just completed a move to be closer to the front lines, and were now just five miles away from "Buke and Vald", which were, of course, actually the single village of Buchenwald.

The Red Cross trucks were huge, and each bore a giant, painted Red Cross logo on its sides and top. Two of the trucks had canvas sides rolled-up to reveal wooden side-benches as transportation for the medical staff. The third truck was all steel, and turned out to be full of fold-up cots, blankets, medical supplies, and special food, including the pap of Gerber's Baby Food, appropriate for starvation victims.

At about the time I could think past my own puking, I noticed that helmets bearing official Red Crosses were strewn about on the ground. Red Cross personnel picked up, wiped off, and put on those helmets; then climbed into their cabs. I assumed that they must have just gone through their own throwing-up routine, tossing helmets off and away from themselves as they quick-exited from their own trucks. (I stress the helmet details, because strangely, during his war, Hitler respected the neutrality of the Red Cross. The helmet was always worn so that the medics would not be mistakenly targeted as soldiers.)

The Master Sergeant turned to the three of us privates recently discharged from the hospital, and, without waiting for our dry heaves to end, told us to climb into his jeep. He told our pick-up driver to go back and stay overnight at the Repple Depple, clean the truck of our vomit, and make himself useful there. He was to come back to The Gate at noon the next day, where the three of us would be waiting for him. Then he was to drive us back to the Repple Depple for our official Army re-assignments.

The Master Sergeant sped his jeep just outside the main compound to an old, free-standing tobacco-shed type of barn, about half as long as a football field. Only he already knew what to expect.

When the rest of us opened the door, the view inside struck us dumb with its ghoulish occupancy.

Chapter 19: The Building of Pure Horror

Image 35: Inside Buchenwald: Ardean R. Miller, US Army Signal Corps

Image 36: Artist Rendering of Shed Exterior

Inside this ill-lit building, two continuous, waist-high counters ran lengthwise, one on each side, leaving a wide center aisle between them. Ignoring the building details, we zeroed in on the sheer, unbridled terror of its bedraggled, emaciated, near-to-death men. They were lying in their own stinking piss and shit and vomit, and were intermixed with the bodies of men who looked just like them, but who had horribly passed into the realm of the dead before our last-minutes-of-hope arrival on the scene. We were looking at about 160 miserably-confined, emaciated men lying side by side on those long counters. Each weighed no more than 55 pounds. The irony was not lost on me: 60 pounds is much too heavy for a field radio…and much too light for a grown man.

Image 37: Artist Rendering of Shed Interior

All heads were positioned toward the center aisle, and one ankle of each prisoner was chain-shackled to the wall. In their feeble condition, even the loudest of their cries was barely audible. About half — randomly mixed throughout — were still alive. Dante himself could never have dreamed up anything more diabolical.

The Master Sergeant, in his uniform which bore chunks of his own recent vomiting, explained to we-3 our job as he had mentally scoped it out.

"First of all, your task is to determine which of these men are dead, and which are still alive." He explained that we were to do this by taking a shaving mirror from our field pack and holding it in front of the mouth and nostril of each successive shackled man. If the mirror fogged, we would know that that prisoner was still breathing and could be saved, a candidate for hands-on liberation, in the truest sense of the word.

As we each reached for our field pack the Sergeant said, "No, the best would be for you (and he pointed to the smallest of the three of us) to do the mirror test on each inmate and use the chain-cutter left behind by the Nazis to free-up those still alive. Push the dead bodies away from them so that by sorting the living from the dead the other two of you can actually do the lifting and carrying, and that'll get the job done faster." He then pointed out one of the windowed doors across the 40-yard-wide strip of grass that separated the back doors of the Building of Pure Horror from the row-houses where the International Red Cross was setting up. He said: "When you've cut the chain and lifted up a freed prisoner, you are to run with him across that strip of grass into the nearest back door, and turn him over to the Red Cross as they direct. Then come running back for the next freed, living man."

What the Master Sergeant said to us teenagers next as I remember it, makes him one of the most brilliant and principled men I have ever met:

"This taste of total hell can either destroy you, or make you into what God wants you to be. At the end of each delivery, as you run back empty-handed for the next close-to-dying man, give thought to what the four of us might commit ourselves to as a Pledge to God at our debriefing tonight.

"You are experiencing pure evil in the raw. If you don't give meaning to the nightmare-filled lives that will surely follow the horrors we're experiencing today, you will have missed the opportunity of a lifetime. Add to your job the reducing of your thoughts to a few simple God-directed words, and we'll agree tonight on what will work best for each of us.

"A famous man once said: 'Evil people destroy us because good people do nothing to stop them.'"

He told us he would check on us during the day and give us further directions at that time. Instructions given, the Master Sergeant, looking green around the gills, stumbled out of the building and back out into the sunlight on that morning of April 11, 1945. I'm sure that in my dazed state I didn't look any better than he.

None of us three teenaged soldiers gave a further thought to our supposed protection as Walking Wounded. Our hearts were bursting with grief. From this moment on, my greatest war wounds would be spiritual, not physical…and I will carry them with me for the rest of my now-numbered days yet to come.

Because the tobacco shed[40] was about 50 yards long, we had 100 yards worth of shoulder-to-shoulder packed men to sort out and at the same time, carry the living to liberation before we ran out of daylight, when blackout would resume.

Image 38: Artist Rendering of Shackle Anchors

Our day's work was cut out for us. Get someone to help us? Where? Every minute counted. We relied only on ourselves. When the first still-living prisoner had been identified by the smaller man, and the chain had been cut, that man found it was no problem at all to push the

---

[40] I describe this building as a tobacco shed based solely on its design and my experience living in the southern US. Though the building may not have been used to dry tobacco, its design strongly resembled those I encountered in the States.

dead bodies away from the living. All moved easily in the slime in which they were mired. We quickly learned that the problem would be its opposite: we could not safely *lift* the slimy living bodies without them slipping out of our arms. I hollered "I'll be right back," and took off running down the aisle to a pile of filthy Nazi blankets I had noticed, grabbed a handful of them and ran back shouting, "Use these to wipe off the slime, so we can get a grip on them for carrying over to the Red Cross Team!"

That worked.

We kept at full speed and hand-liberated about 80 surviving men just in time to beat the sunset. If those blankets had not been there, we would never have finished in time. Our triumph for the still-living was not complete, however. Two of the men died in my arms before I could run the 40 yards to their awaiting Red Cross cots.

At sundown, the Master Sergeant rejoined us. Our minds blown by doing what no men should ever have to do, the four of us discussed and composed our Pledge. The Master Sergeant raised his hand skyward, and we followed his lead, saying in unison: "**We Will Devote Our Lives to Helping People to Understand Each Other Better.**" Although the four of us have had no contact since, The Pledge still drives me now at age 86.

Sunlight gone, the Master Sergeant used his slit-rigged flashlight to lead us to the row-houses that had so recently served as the posh headquarters for the Buchenwald Gestapo. Those would be our accommodations for the night.

Each of us solved our bathing problem in his own way. The cleansing process involved two stages: cleaning our bodies, and cleaning our clothes. The only clothes we had were the uniforms on our backs when discharged from the hospital. My solution was to take the shower while still dressed, scrub the fabric, toss it on the bathroom's tile floor, and *then* scrub my body. I then re-dressed with one garment at a time, wearing it inside out, so I could scrub its other surface. Once each garment was thus thoroughly cleaned on both sides, I took it off, wrung it out, and threw it onto a clean section of tile. Finally, I completely re-dressed in a uniform borrowed for me by the Master Sergeant, leaving mine to dry and be inherited by others. But I never parted with my special padded long-john underwear. I hand carried them until dry.

Afterwards, we met in a small parlor, and the Master Sergeant debriefed us. We let our hair down over a supper of Army K rations chow. What we had done together that horror-filled day, and The Pledge to God we had made together as we had finished-up at sundown, had dissolved all our differences in rank, age, and backgrounds into the commonality of purpose that transcended pecking order. As he finished up our debriefing, our leader asked if any of us had any questions.

"Do we get to see General Patton before our ride back to the Repple Depple tomorrow?" I asked. The Master Sergeant paused as if weighing a decision, but only momentarily.

"General Patton is a legend. He is loyal to his staff, and we are loyal to him. But because I suspect that all four of us will carry a forever-burden of nightmares from this day forward, I must answer accurately, and from my heart.

"If you ever tell anyone I said this, I will deny it.

"But, despite my repeated pleadings to the General in our daily phone call briefings, he is not yet here. I have no idea when or if he will come. If he doesn't, General Eisenhower will have to appoint someone to assume overall command here, and do it quickly. Tomorrow, this place will probably be swarming with newspaper columnists and radio commentators, and the poor ex-prisoners, with no place to go, will become victims of another kind. This hell-hole will remain a hell-hole, until someone with leadership clout takes hold of it.

"By now, you may have already guessed... *It was I who summoned you here.*

"Once I heard the distress radio calls from Buchenwald, I knew that getting you and the Red Cross here in a red-hot hurry was too damn important to wait for any more discussion. I've worked in General Patton's headquarters ever since Normandy, some ten months ago. I know well his distinctive, high-pitched voice, and imitating it for giving orders to the Repple Depple was a piece of cake. I've never done such a thing before, but I didn't have to think twice about doing it today."

Incredible.

If anybody ever qualified as being a first-rate, humane, brilliant problem-solver, it was the Master Sergeant. Thinking about it awhile later — and noting additional accounts over the years — here's how I put all the pieces together:

For several days prior to our arrival, the Nazi guards could hear the big guns of the advancing American Third Army getting closer and closer. Many of those guards, wanting nothing to do with being captured at the incriminating scene of Buchenwald, had run for their lives.

Some of the remaining guards — in a desperate attempt to keep surviving prisoners from contact with liberating Allies — threatened to force the able-bodied prisoners to march out with them. Once en route, the force-marched prisoners could be more conveniently exterminated by bullets or exhaustion. But with the preliminary thinning of the guards, the timing was also right for the prisoners' activity of their own.

One of the inmates was a Polish engineer named Gwidon Damazyn. Somehow, in his several years as prisoner, Damazyn had built seven radio receivers in collaboration with Russian prisoners of war who had started an underground resistance movement. Working alongside fellow Pole Teofil Witek and German radio technician Helmut Wagner, he had also built a shortwave radio transmitter.[41]

However, after the discovery of a similar device at Mittelbau-Dora Concentration Camp led the SS to conduct a search for transmitters at other camps, the Buchenwald resistance fighters felt it necessary to destroy their transmitter. A new device was built on April 8, and they were able to send a transmission. There is no clear indication as to who composed the message, only that it was put together by the leaders of the resistance movement.

Witek described the events surrounding the transmission as follows. On April 8, in the movie room (where the transmitter was located) a distress call for help was sent using Morse code in Russian, English, and German. Witek's account has it taking place around noon on April 8th; other accounts have it taking place overnight between April 8th and 9th. Damazyn sent the English and German transmissions, and a Russian prisoner of war named Konstantin Ivanovich Leonov sent the Russian transmission.

Meanwhile, Patton's Headquarters was just completing a move to be closer to the front lines. His radio operator would have been startled to receive this out-of-the-blue message — startled because radios of that day were line-of-sight. If the tip of the antenna of one field radio

---

[41] Details of the underground resistance movement and their hidden transmitters, as well as their SOS message and its response, were provided by the dedicated reference staff of the Boston Public Library. See Acknowledgments and Bibliographic References.

had been blocked by a hill or a building from seeing the tip of the other antenna, they could not have communicated without an arranged intermediary between them. The distress message had to be coming from somewhere in line-of-sight proximity to the Headquarters' new location. Furthermore, as a radio man myself, I know that they would both have to be on the same frequency setting. If the inmates addressed their urgent message to General Patton's Army on exactly the right frequency, they must have had an informant who kept them up to date on troop movements in the area. Someone had to be slipping notes, or otherwise passing information, into and out of Buchenwald for both inmate leaders and Third Army Intelligence.

Normally, in the Third Army office along with the radio operator, there would have been two key personnel with their desks nearby: Patton's number one Operations man (who would have been an officer), and Patton's number one Administrative man (who would have held the non-officer position of master sergeant and was thus outranked by the Operations man).

Patton's radio operator would have immediately referred the prisoners' cry for help to the Operations man. However, if that officer had stepped away from his desk, the radio man would have referred the distress signal to Patton's top Administrative person, our Master Sergeant. The English translation of the message was this:

"To the Allies. To the army of General Patton. This is the Buchenwald concentration camp. SOS. We request help. They want to evacuate us. The SS wants to destroy us."

The multilingual transmissions were sent in several waves; according to one report, up to twelve times. Upon hearing this desperate plea, the Master Sergeant would have told the radio operator to reply to the prisoners immediately, and what to say.

After listening for three minutes, Damazyn received the following response in English Morse code:

"KZ Bu. [Buchenwald concentration camp]. Hold out. Rushing to your aid. Staff of Third Army."

Damazyn is said to have fainted after receiving the message.

For the Buchenwald prisoners desperately awaiting radio response, receiving this reply quickly would have been huge. It verified that the Third Army was indeed close by, and that they were interested in helping out. Thus encouraged, the better-fed inmates are reported to have stormed the watchtowers, killed the remaining guards, and self-liberated the camp[42]. They broke the locks on the kitchens and the food stores, and doled out food to the weaker prisoners, likely knowing from bitter experience that emaciated, starved people could not just stuff themselves without risking instantaneous death. They opened The Gate and sat and waited for the Third Army Command to come and tell them what to do next.

Immediately after drafting and sending his reply, the Master Sergeant would have directed the radio operator to switch his frequency to the land-line connection: he had to talk to General Patton immediately. The Master Sergeant told us that he had repeated the urgency message to General Patton during their early morning status reports on the 10th and 11th. Having committed to helping the desperate prisoners, the Master Sergeant must have now become desperate himself.

Although he had no idea what to expect at Buchenwald, he knew he would have to be bold enough to scrounge up a few men who could help out. As an administrator, re-deploying official troops for his own private mission would have been unthinkable. But he *could* contact the Replacement Depot to check for the prospect of fresh, incoming men. Although the three of us just discharged from the hospital hardly qualified as "fresh troops", we did come with one crucial recommendation: we were between official assignments, and therefore bureaucratically available to anyone with enough balls, resourcefulness, and commitment to grab us.

That's when he radioed the Repple Depple, impersonating Patton.

Knowing his boss better than almost anybody else, and braced by his own sense of urgency, he found it easy to intimidate the poor buck sergeant on the other end of the line.

Without knowing whether any other Allied soldiers had already made it there, on the 11th, knowing that the three of us en route would need on-site direction, the Master Sergeant jeeped over to Buchenwald to scope things out for himself. What he saw in the main camp had to have changed his life forever. There were over *24,000* prisoners (including the 9,000-plus that had just survived the over-thirty-mile forced march from Ohrdruf, and excluding the 900 shot along the way). Most of the living were in a state of animation-in-limbo: those still men-

---

[42] Though I was too stunned to have noticed at the time, the Nazis at Buchenwald feared that the first liberators would be the Russian army. In anticipation (in order to minimize retribution), they had started taking better care of the Russian prisoners.

tating realized they were no longer intimidated by Nazi guards, but they also had no place to go.

All alone, the Master Sergeant was helpless to deal with the sheer scale of stench and misery that he had discovered at Buchenwald. Somehow though, through his own retching, he had been selfless enough to discover the Building of Pure Horror that lay outside the regular fencing (and that Main Camp inmates may never have been aware of). Here was something a few men could do something about! The three of us from the Repple Depple, plus an International Red Cross Unit came together just in time to become his temporary "army".

Once our debriefing was over, the Master Sergeant concluded with:

"From now 'til noon tomorrow, when your truck arrives, you're on your own. Be glad that you will be picked up and on your way to somewhere else, away from this horrible smell of human decay and offal, and the sights from a nation gone crazy that will haunt you for the rest of your lives.

"Don't miss that pick-up truck! Maybe you'll be assigned to some nice place to sit out the rest of this War, and won't have to be among those poor bastards tasked with storming the beaches of Japan. Good luck, and get some sleep, if you can."

The next day, when the advance units of the Third Army came streaming through the Main Gate, the Master Sergeant neatly finished-up the one-shot humanitarian work that he had started, and disappeared out of my life — a true hero in every sense of the word. I am sorry that his heroism has been unsung until now. If he is alive today, he is over 100 years old.

I remember wondering what the shackled, emaciated men in that shed had done to be so heinously treated by the Nazis. As a Jewish-raised 19-year-old boy, the shock at the time certainly precluded my putting it all together. It turns out that these most horribly treated prisoners were not Jews. As later clarified, Buchenwald was much more of a death camp for political enemies than for Jews. Records remind us that Nazi extermination included five million non-Jews, as well as six million Jews. But of these many millions of people, nothing could have been a more compelling lesson for us than hand-carrying just 80 of them — no matter who they were.

What could the *non-Jews* we found in the Building of Pure Horror have done to merit chain-shackling and deliberate, systematic teetering on starvation? What drives men to do this to each other?

And what happens to those who get stuck having to witness it?

Chapter 20: Nocturnal Visitor

For that one night, we each had a privately assigned, deluxe, former-Gestapo row-house bedroom (wow!). But I found myself fitfully awake after that day which my mind would never let end. It was dark. All buildings were blacked-out, there were still Nazi planes in the air, and I was exhausted out of my skull, so there was really nothing else to do but to stay in bed and try to get a night's sleep. Hah! Fat chance.

First there were the nightmares and the stench. There was no way to shut either of them off. Even the extreme fatigue, and its roaring accompanying headaches, alternately had me sleeping and waking as I headed into that God-forsaken night. That I could sleep at all was thanks to all the horror-conditioning I had undergone in the endless battle campaigns before.

Against this backdrop of total physical and mental exhaustion, sometime in the middle of the night, I realized that one of my doors was open. Someone had turned on the light. I found myself hyped to a state of full-awareness from my unstable condition. It was the separation of reality from nightmare dream. Then there was my focus on a real intruder.

There was a pajama-clad man in my room and, arms extended, he was headed for the bed. (Pajamas? Who wore pajamas?) There was no question that it was a man, because his private parts were hanging out, and he was in a state of full erection. It was my one and only experience in a man-to-man sex-approach situation, and my reaction was more combat-honed instinct than reasoning response. As he approached my bed, I reached for, and levered a round into my M-1 carbine:

"The first shot goes through the ceiling, and the next one blows off your kneecap! You have 5 seconds to turn around and get the hell out of here!" He could tell that, sleep-drugged or not, I meant business. He turned around and left through the balcony door.

I got up, went to the bathroom and tried to throw up again (which I couldn't), turned the light back out in my blacked-out room, and paced the floor until finally fatigue overcame me once again, and I stumbled back to bed.

The next morning, there was a knock on my door. I opened it to see a tech sergeant standing there.

"I have come to apologize for my Lieutenant. You have to realize that the dead bodies and the living skeletons and the stench that we saw and smelled on our way into here yesterday had gotten us reeling, and he has been under pressure… tremendous pressure. I can assure you that his sexual preference has not taken away his efficiency as a human being."

"I have no prejudice against anyone's sexual orientation. I admire your devotion to him and agree with you that the pressures on us all are enormous. This is a Murder Camp for God sakes! (I remember that being the first time I spoke that thought out loud.)

"Tell him that I forgive him completely. I will be leaving here at noon for re-assignment, and I am certain that our paths will never cross again. If they do, there will be no mention of what happened last night."

We said goodbye, and he closed the door.

Chapter 21: A Guided Tour of Evil

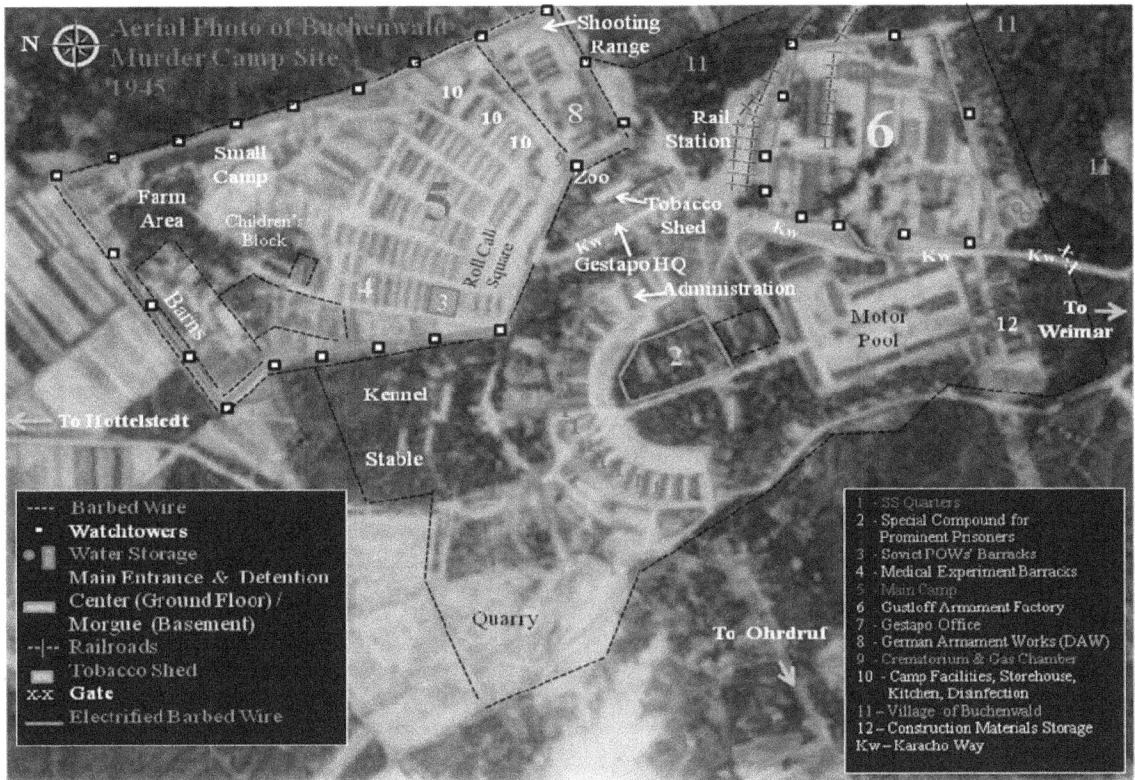

Image 39: Buchenwald Aerial Map Overlay

I began April 12, 1945 by walking around in the area near The Gate. The camp was encircled on the outside by barbed wire. Inside that perimeter, a second layer of barbed wire was attached to posts by telltale insulated fasteners at twenty foot intervals. This was an electrified wire such as those used to pen-in cattle. I was not about to test its efficacy by touching it.

The big difference from the day before was that the whole area was now crawling with American soldiers (I had noticed only us a mere day ago). Even though The Gate was open, the former prisoners were walking around inside. There was no place to go, the war was still on, and there was no one to turn to for information about family or friends.

As I walked, a healthy-looking man in prison garb blazoned with the Star-of-David matched my pace, and offered to take me on a walking tour of The Camp. I wondered why he had chosen me.

Looking back, my appearance must have been unique: I was dressed in a clean uniform, topped by a hospital-issue brand-new American soldier's helmet. I still had no unit-patch on my shoulder, because I had yet to be re-assigned. The clean new pack on my back (which I had retrieved from the Master Sergeant's jeep at day's end and held it away from my slime-covered uniform until showering later), and an M-1 carbine (not a rifle) on my under-padded shoulder singled me out as being different from the other American soldiers who had a look-alike orderliness, reflecting the military groups in which they were clustered. I had explained to him that I was on my own, my assignment finished. I told him about the last many hours, from the saving of almost hopeless lives to the scrubbing of my clothes.

He, in turn, told me a little about himself, especially that he had enjoyed privileged status because of his perfect command of New York State's colloquial English. He had a Brooklyn accent, which impressed the Nazis as particularly authentic. On his part, intercepting and translating radio communications from American and English forces operating across Western Europe was an extremely valuable asset to the Gestapo, so he had been unrestricted in his movements about The Camp and was still alive because he had carefully nurtured a reputation for otherwise minding his own business. He did not seem conflicted about serving in this way, and I don't blame him. We didn't discuss it, but it would have been obvious that if he didn't serve in this capacity, someone else would have. He was just bursting with information, and wanted someone to share it with.

My guide (whose name I do not remember) and I went down a trail. Starting inside The Gate and over to the right, I saw an area containing three buildings: Reception, Extermination, and Crematorium.

Reception and Decontamination

The railroad track entering the compound from the east was the end of the line for thousands and thousands of Buchenwald arrivals who had been routed there from all over Europe. For illustration purposes, let's look at a trainload of such arrivals who have not come from other camps, but directly from citizenship abruptly terminated by Gestapo arrest. Consider that they have been unilaterally declared guilty, and were now arriving at the Buchenwald rail yards as fresh meat.

When these ill-fated human beings stumbled, exhausted and befouled, out of the jam-packed railroad cars, and were herded into the roll-call area of The Main Camp, the infamous finger-point selection process took place. An SS Nazi thug would send some to the right and to their execution, and others to the left to become slave laborers. A wave of the hand thus determined who would live and who would die. Why prisoners were sent to the left or right was never explained to them…and as they never saw each other again, they could not learn from one another through the grapevine.

My guide said that he had often seen these segregation events. Children, the infirm, or the elderly always went to the right, sometimes with, but most often without, those who loved them. At Buchenwald, if you were adult and able-bodied Jewish, Romani (Gypsy), homosexual, or other such-listed minorities, there was another line straight ahead especially for you. That mix was sent to The Small Camp within The Main Camp, where you were isolated for export via a forced march, or otherwise moved to what the Nazis called Class I Camps — those specially dedicated to the complete murder of an entire people (as the Nazis famously put it, "The Ultimate Solution to the Jewish Problem").

Buchenwald was Gestapo-designated as a Class II Camp, which was devoted to the elimination of political prisoners and other extra-special Enemies of the State. Once again, for Jews and non-Jews alike, it is worth recalling that while six million Jews were being murdered, so too were five million non-Jews. Buchenwald was a key camp in this part of The Holocaust.

The pathway to the right (and therefore to death) led to a group of barracks buildings, because the number entering The Main Camp was large enough that most times they could not all be gassed and cremated in one group. The meticulous Nazi record-keepers assigned each new prisoner a number, whether or not the Nazis had time to tattoo them on the victims' forearms before gassing them.

Those sent to the left ended up at a different group of barracks buildings. They were soon issued uniforms, with or without ID patches, and all would have numbers tattooed on their arms.

The path straight ahead, which led to the holding area known as The Small Camp, led to a fixed size barracks, which therefore varied from nearly empty to jam-packed overflowing.

These inmates were all tattooed, issued uniforms, and had identifying patches sewn onto their prison garb.

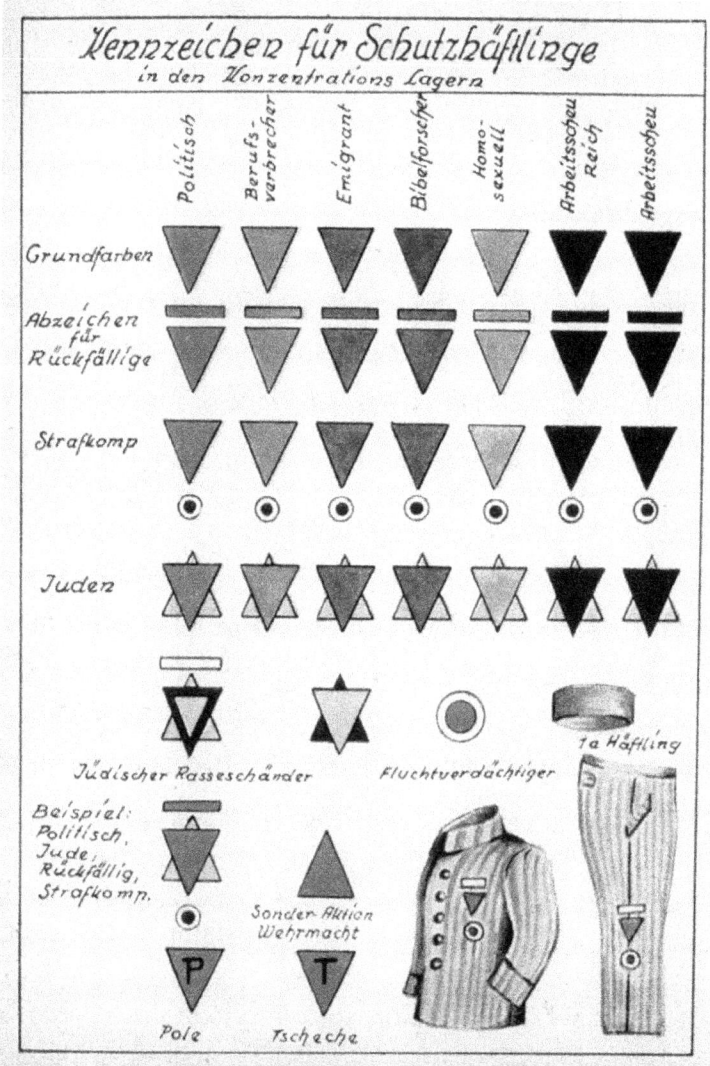

Image 40: Prison Badge Poster

For all prisoner categories, decontamination was essential, so that whatever disease and infections they carried with them did not spread to the rest of the camp and its precious Gestapo cadres (the Nazis' confidence in their superiority stopped short of being carefree about the dangers of typhus and other contagion). Whether newly arrived prisoners were slated to be murdered or not, all were decontaminated as quickly as possible.

Extermination: The Gas Chamber at Buchenwald

The filthy traveling clothes that prisoners had on their backs were, by this time, reeking. The prisoners were told to strip, that their clothes were going to be laundered, sorted out, and later returned. They were then told to enter the shower room to cleanse themselves.

Imagine walking in unclothed: men and women and children all nude. It was a monstrous thing, but they had already learned that the Nazis were monsters and they probably considered the thoughtfulness of granting them cleanliness as an unexpected boon. (I say probably because none ever survived, of course.) It was calculated that many willingly walked into their execution chamber, the doors were closed, and the poison gas was either thrown into the area from canisters, or introduced from vents in the ceiling.

The most salient feature that I saw inside the Crematorium was the irregular mural design, in tones of red and grey, that some Futuristic Artist might have randomly painted from 5 to 9 feet off the floor, with enough excess to allow the paint to run down.

My guide explained that the "artists" had, in fact, been the victims of gassing. The walls were rough, and the color had come from the blood of their clawing fingertips, ranging from the reach-height of a small child to that of the tallest adults. He pointed out that the inmates often believed the Nazi guards' spiel that this was a Shower Building. Even once inside, and seeing blood-stain-created futuristic art on the walls, I could see how — having been so long terrified in transit — prisoners could still buy into the fiction that they were going to be clean at last…maybe even billeted in those nice new buildings (whose grounds had been kept clean by their enslaved prisoners).

After slaughter in the gas chamber and before cremation, the dead victims' jaws were smashed, in order to extract the teeth for their precious gold fillings.

Prisoner Barracks and Roll Call Square

From the Gas Chamber, you could see the buildings that had held tens of thousands of inmates. They were uniform in design, laid out carefully and all built to the same blueprint. Being eight years old or less, they were fresh and new. Between them was Roll Call Square.

Image 41: Prisoner Barracks at Buchenwald

My guide laid out the routine for me. Those who would be working in the fields, for example, were sub-divided into which field they were assigned for the day. Leaders would meticulously enter the data into that day's work sheet. Every single prisoner had to be accounted for when the day was over, or else. As shown in the map at the beginning of this chapter, there were stables, quarry, kennels, barns, and a farm area. Outside of the main fence, unmarked, were other fields and buildings.

Crematorium

Image 42: The Ovens of Buchenwald

My guide explained that the ovens were each single-body capacity only, which meant that they — not the numbers gassable at one time — were the limiting factor at Buchenwald. He added that when the ovens were in full operation, the smoke was black, and that it was common for chunks of scorched or burning flesh to come out within the smoke. It was very probable that there was no odor of decaying bodies, because they would not have been standing for days, as were the ones we saw. Instead, burned while still fresh, the odor was that of scorched meat.

By the time I saw the wagon path from the gas chamber to the crematorium, there was an accumulated pile of decaying bodies lying on the ground, abandoned when fuel was no longer available to burn them up. Added to this was another wagon loaded with special corpses stacked like so much firewood. Shortages of all kinds, including crematoria fuel, were the result of massive bomb raids as the Americans and British achieved mastery of the skies.

My guide said that there was no question that villagers in Buchenwald smelled the burnt flesh from the smokestack, and readily identified the Crematorium from which it had come. All knew that there was no animal rendering there, and that the chunks of flesh were from streams of murdered human beings. They knew, but they must have been used to it…

The Zoo

Image 43: The Bear's Den at Buchenwald

Some of what looks like buildings in an aerial photo were actually fenced-in pens for the camp director's toy: a collection of animals. The most famous of these animal pits was the one containing two huge bears.

My private guide pointed out that the bodies in that location bore damaged skulls for a very special reason at Buchenwald. The camp's last Commandant, after breakfast and before starting his working day, walked the few dozen yards from his office over to the Bears' Den to enjoy watching the bears tear apart and eat the body of a prisoner who had been killed by clubbing, instead of gassing. This was to protect the bears from accidental poisoning by eating human meat tainted with Zyklon-B gas chemicals. Surely, this would have been unacceptable cruelty to animals…

Manufacturing

Inside the first "manufacturing" facility that we went to, I saw two buckets filled with human teeth. My guide pointed out that these buckets were en route to another building for harvesting the gold they contained. There, they were heated to the point at which molten gold would run out from the bottom of a crucible, to be gathered in ceramic buckets.

Image 44: Teeth from the Prisoners of Buchenwald

In those days, only gold was used for tooth repair, and its uniformly high carat content was changed into world market monies by the Swiss Banks — Swiss neutrality being respected by all the world's nations (to their financial benefit). This was a meaningful source of funding for Hitler's war machine, and therefore reason enough for Nazi victims to be twice-violated, and twice-robbed: victims were murdered, and then beaten; their teeth stolen, and then robbed of their precious metal. The resulting flow of gold funded much of the destruction that followed my path through the war, from the battlefields where Allied soldiers died all around me to the events which led wounded me to the very gates of Buchenwald itself.

The other "manufacturing facility" at Buchenwald housed the organized process for rendering human skin into the translucent parchment used for making lampshades. My guide had not personally seen the skinning room where the selected dead bodies were processed, but he was witness to slave laborers walking across the open space, carrying folded stacks of the parchment into the area where the lampshades were fabricated.

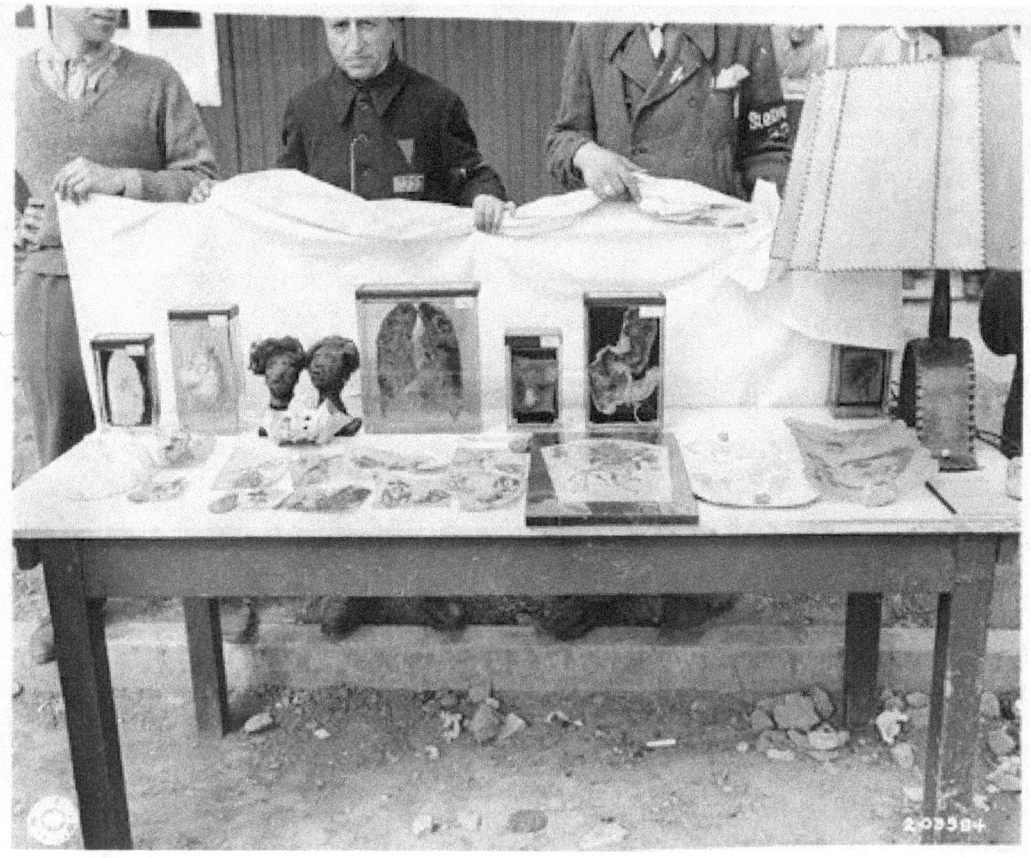

Image 45: Lampshades of Human Skin

Today, Buchenwald has been transformed into a museum, and its current Memorial Room is where pre-cremation bodies were skinned for making parchment. In The Workroom, which I saw on my tour that day, I saw many folded parchment samples in stacks. The awaiting lampshade wire frames and manufacturing jigs were indications of organized production activity. Such depravity is beyond all humane understanding.

The American soldier, upon entering Germany in 1945, walked into a situation where the Nazi empire was falling apart and the civilian population knew it. There was justifiable universal fear that when the true nature of the Holocaust became known, the German people would be at extreme risk of retaliation from a world horrified by a population that had allowed and abetted such extreme callous treatment of their fellow human beings. A way of escape for the young and middle-aged female population would be to marry an American soldier, and thus be an American citizen, and post-war be free to emigrate to re-join her husband in the USA, land of opportunity.

From the soldier's point of view, his life was in extreme danger from the Nazi armies that gave no indication whatsoever of giving up the fight. The result was as to be expected from women of little hope and men of little hope, in a leaderless environment. The gift of a beautiful lampshade was an ideal icebreaker for a sex-starved frightened soldier and the ladies in desperate situations in the surrounding communities. A hundred lampshades could have disappeared in an eye wink in the four days between our liberating the tobacco shed and when General Patton finally arrived to the chaos at that Camp.

The one remaining area that my Jewish guide had prioritized for me was The Small Camp.

Image 46: The Small Camp at Buchenwald

This was a destitute, grungy section within The Main Camp. According to figures released later, it held 4,000 people when I was there, only half of them Jews bearing the Star of David. The other half of The Small Camp bore a symbol which I later learned identified them as Other Undesirables, in this instance, Romani (Gypsies). Because of their just-completed forced march together on below-subsistence rations, they were in a condition of unbelievable squalor — well below the physical condition of that The Main Camp inmates.

At noon, my guide and I positioned ourselves just outside the main gate, where my other two liberation buddies and the Master Sergeant were already waiting for the 4x4 truck that was due at any minute.

The driver was ashen-faced from the small visual sight of stacked bodies, and the huge pervasive stink of Buchenwald that he had gotten once again just by driving up to The Gate. Looking at the Master Sergeant, I knew that he, too, was as devastated as I by our mutual experience.

Although non-commissioned officers don't rate a salute, the three of us fired off to our adoptive Master Sergeant what was surely the sharpest military salute in history. We boarded our 4x4, and headed down the short road to our little Repple Depple...this time at a safe speed.

Chapter 22: Back to the Repple Depple

We arrived to find a couple dozen men like ourselves. We-3 didn't do much talking to the others, or even to each other as I awaited my first official assignment since being hospitalized three months prior.

As we waited, my mind slipped into some of the many unanswered questions from Buchenwald. What was the future for those I had saved: the forty, 50–60 pound men I had carried at a run, one-by-slippery-and-stinking-one within my slippery-and-stinking arms from the Tobacco Shed to the former deluxe Gestapo Headquarters Red Cross facility 40 yards away? Each time I set one carefully down on his nice clean Red Cross cot, I asked myself "What was his history? What so-called crimes led him to this? And what are his chances of recovering with his sanity intact?"

Unbelievably, only three days earlier, I was still saying goodbye to people at the hospital. But already, *everything* from my pre-Buchenwald era was a lifetime ago…

The next morning, the Repple Depple buck sergeant handed us our file folders, and said that because of my radio background, I was being sent to fill a Code Red Emergency position desperately phoned in that morning. I was assigned to something called the 225th Anti-aircraft Searchlight Battalion, which I had never heard of. No surprise there: such battalions required mobility independent of frontline priorities. Their job was to go wherever Allied cities were under air attack (*e.g.*, London, Le Havre, Antwerp), so they could shoot down Nazi Luftwaffe airplanes. For that reason, the 225th got its assignments directly from Eisenhower's Headquarters, known as SHAEF[43].

While waiting for my transport, I saw the other two teen-agers who had been with me for the life-changing experience at Buchenwald get on a 6x6 together. We've never seen or heard from each other since. I don't remember their first names, though we probably addressed each other that way for our brief time together. For all of us, there were many fellow soldiers that we knew only for a day or two.

---

[43] This was pronounced "Shayf", acronym for Supreme Headquarters, Allied Expeditionary Force.

I was told which truck to board to get to my next destination. For that entire journey I was preoccupied. The Buchenwald questions reared, and reared again, multiplying with each round: What are the chances of the Tobacco Shed victims recovering with their sanity intact? What reduced their captors to becoming such practitioners of evil? What will become of these torturers, if returned to society? What if they *aren't*? And what becomes of a world that allows such tragedies to exist, fester, and thrive while doing nothing better than looking the other way and hoping for the best?

Ultimately I asked Him the million-dollar question: "What kind of a God are You who could allow such things to happen in His world?" And then its recoil question jarred back at me just as hard: "Is it *His* job to get it right in this world…or *ours?*"

To this day, I sometimes explode awake in a confusing mixture: still drugged by a fresh nightmare, and responding with an un-aimable rush of adrenaline. And though I have long since grown to become a practicing Christian as well as a Jew, in those moments, I still ask The Big Questions. "What kind of a God are You?" and "Is it *Your* job to get it right…or *mine?*"

I had plenty of introspection time during transit to dwell on these questions, and to internalize my answers. Upon my arrival in Holland on the afternoon of April 13th, however, that think-time came to a screeching halt.

Chapter 23: From Radio to Switchboard

I was assigned to round out a three-man crew living at a railroad switching yard ten miles outside of the Dutch city of Maastricht. Our house was a pyramidal tent, and our crew comprised an Anti-aircraft Gunner, a Searchlight-shiner, and me. Their single-gun-and-light emplacement was at the western end of a temporary pontoon bridge on the western shore of the Maas River. The bombed-out ruins of the permanent bridge were sticking up out of the river nearby. Our armies held a beachhead deep into Nazi Germany on the eastern end.

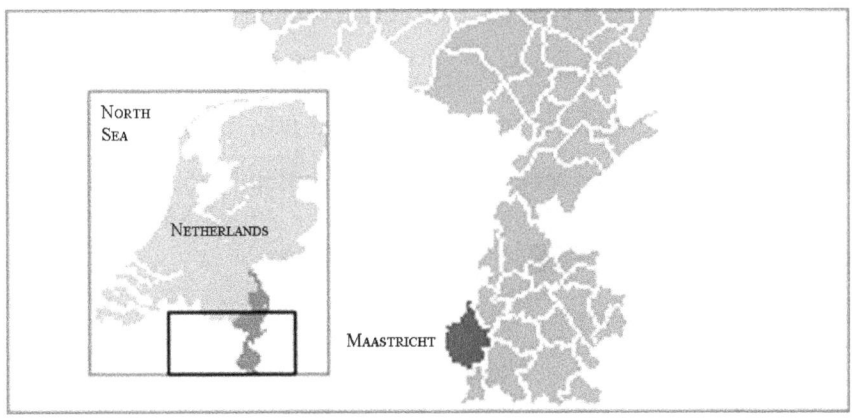

Image 47: Location of Maastricht

After shaking hands all around, I was immediately sent alone by US-military train to downtown Maastricht. I was a working passenger on that shuttle, paying my way by shoveling coal into the engine's boiler from the attached coal car.

Maastricht, because of its special geographical location, had been liberated before the rest of the Dutch homeland. When I got there, I found a beautiful, intact, old Dutch city, miraculously spared bombing and shelling[44] by either side because of a unique, non-critical geographical location. This was a good-sized community, now double its pre-war population of 100,000 because of escapees from nearby still-Nazi-held parts of Holland. After four years of occupation, this area was now safely on the side of the angels (us Allies). The Nazis were only 20 miles away on the other side of the river, and for much of the time, all of the long-distance

---

[44] Bombs are deployed from the air; shells are deployed from the ground.

civilian phone lines had been down. Each of the telephone land-lines was repeatedly broken by the enemy in dozens of places. To remedy this communication chaos, the US Army had installed a switchboard to receive all remaining local civilian lines, as well as the only trunk into Maastricht from the outside world. This trunk, which snaked modestly along the ground into my building, connected the switchboard directly to General Eisenhower's headquarters in Paris.

As a trained radio operator, my job was to cover the night shift on that switchboard. I received on-the-job training from the daytime guy, and then took over at 2200 hours (10 p.m.) on April 13 for my first 12-hour hitch manning a busy, busy American military switchboard that also interfaced with the newly-freed City Government offices. I had used that same equipment in radio school back in the USA, so the technical aspects were a piece of cake. But thankfully, the transition to new place, new people, and new responsibilities left me way too busy to think about the horrors I had recently witnessed in that Nazi murder camp. Whew!

Image 48: Switchboard Operator August 1943

On the night shift that began on April 13th and lasted to April 14th, I was on my first independent switchboard duty. Every trunk line call from anywhere stopped with me, unless I patched it in to another line. Every place that could call me was represented by its own plug-in hole, covered by a little metal plate hinged at the bottom. When a caller turned a hand crank at their end, a surge of reverse-polarity electricity negated the magnetism holding their metal plate in place, letting it flop down to expose the hole. (There were a handful of civilian holes, but most were military.) Once I got an incoming call, I manually plugged it in to the right destination circuit, whether completing a civilian-to-civilian call, or a military one straight to General Eisenhower's Paris Headquarters. So there were maybe 50 metal-plate-covered outlets on the switchboard, and when one of those hinged metal plates flopped down, it did so with a distinctive "click". At night when I got drowsy and things were quiet, I would fall asleep at the switchboard (we used to say, "Fall asleep at the switch, bored!"). I doubt I lost any calls, though, because I became quickly attuned to that "click", which awoke me with a start.

Sometime after midnight of my first shift: "Click!"

"Uh-oh," I startle to my wits. "An incoming from SHAEF[45]!" I plug into it.

"This is Private Arnold. Who's this?"

"This is Colonel So-and-So from SHAEF headquarters."

"Yes, sir!"

"I have the sad duty to inform you that President Roosevelt has died."

I was blown away…no one even knew that FDR[46] was seriously ill. (For strategic reasons, it had been a well-kept secret. For security, there was also some delay before contacting me with that sensitive information.) Franklin Roosevelt had been elected President four times, and in office since the depth of the Great Depression. He had long been our Commander-in-Chief, and losing him now at such a crucial time in the second World War was unthinkable. I thought (hoped even) that somebody was playing a rumor game. Perhaps someone had cut into our land line…they were doing that all the time. I pressed for validation.

---

[45] At this point, General Eisenhower's headquarters was located in Paris.
[46] Franklin Delano Roosevelt, USA's beloved 32nd President.

"Sir, would you please verify this?" He gave me the day's correct code.

"Yes, sir, ready for orders!"

"I want you to notify the Burgomeister (mayor) immediately."

"Yes, sir!"

FDR was much beloved across the world, and nowhere more than here: the Roosevelts were of Dutch ancestry ("Roosenfelt"). My job was to notify this blacked-out town that their incredible hero had died.

I plugged into the Burgomeister. In the daytime, you could see right across the square. I was on one side of the square in a town office, and across the square you could see the city hall complex. It was a gorgeous building of decorative multi-colored bricks, and it had survived both World Wars.

Image 49: Maastricht City Hall 2008

The town officials were on 24-hour call, sleeping in their offices in this long rectangular administration building with lots of windows. Nothing but blackness that night, though, as befitted a town complying with the mandate to make it hard for enemy planes to see bombing targets at night.

I plugged in and cranked the ringer handle. The Burgomeister himself answered. (His phone was at his bedside, as were those of all the city officials who slept right in their offices during those months of acute crisis.)

"Ja?"

"Herr Burgomeister, this is Private Arnold on the switchboard... It is my sad duty to inform you that President Roosevelt has died."

"Oh, mein Gott!"

The mayor spoke English well, but in reaction to the overwhelming gravity of the situation, he instinctively reverted to his own tongue. I had to give him the proper codes to verify that the news was real, just as I had required of SHAEF.

Within a few moments, I saw a candle light up in his room across the way. Under strict blackout, that was a no-no; but out of respect for a much beloved man, he lit a candle. And then I saw, in the room to the right, another candle. Then in the room to the left. He must have told his two chief aides to spread the news, each on his own side of the building — because in each window successively to the right and to the left, more candles lit up as the news spread. The emotions within me, a guy who had spent all of my life from age seven with Roosevelt as President, were akin to theirs. And to see the whole town lighting up in spite of the blackout curfew as the word went around town…it was just an incredible sight.

Then all the citizens, as they learned the news, poured out of their homes, most also carrying a candle. The square, and the streets leading to it from every direction, became jammed and brightly illuminated. Most of the citizens had also donned the black arm-bands of mourning. (So many in Holland had had loved ones die in the four years of warfare that there were plenty of arm-bands to go around.) Most were also mourning aloud.

That forbidden illumination, and the accompanying keening, told me volumes about global connections that remain within my heart today.

Chapter 24: Mistresses, Rations, and Jazz

When I got off my first 12-hour night shift at 10 a.m., shoveling coal for my train ride "home" was the cap-off for being flat-out tired, so a big chunk of my day was spent sleeping in our three-man pyramidal tent.

But I didn't stay asleep until my next shift.

The day operator who had shown me the ropes when I first reported to the switchboard not only explained my official role; he explained a couple of unofficial ones, as well.

It seems that the prior night-shift man had had a mistress in town. As his legacy, he wished for the replacement man to look in on her. This was not about the crude, attempted passing of a lonely girl from one army buddy to another. It was about something brighter in the midst of war. Although Maastricht had been spared destruction by bombs, its people knew well the deprivations brought by world conflict. Good food was in short supply. When the prior night-shift man visited his mistress in town, he would bring along Army food as a supplement for her and her two small children. I had replaced him in his official role, and though I had never met him, I resolved to comply with his request for my fulfilling an unofficial role, too. Although I was to be on the switchboard for only two nights, I stayed in touch with his mistress and her kids for the three weeks I remained in the Maastricht area.

There was another unofficial legacy. My predecessor was not only a radio man like me, but he had also belonged to a pick-up jazz group called The Netherlanders. The day-shift man mentioned it when orienting me, explaining that when my predecessor got reassigned, the jazz group had found itself without a sax player.

"Wait a minute!" I exclaimed. "*I* play the sax! But…I don't have one here."

"Never mind that, neither did he. They'll lend you one." Sure enough, the other guys were happy to have me.

And so it was: every afternoon I climbed aboard the train with my stash of Army food, and waved good-bye to my tent-mates. I shoveled coal for the 10 miles westward to Maastricht, and stopped in at the house of my predecessor's girlfriend.

These visits might seem strange to you now, but a man who was so far surviving the War when so many around him weren't is full of thoughts. Part of him is constantly looking for something — *anything* — that he can make sense of. Something that he can make right. I was already head-over-heels in love with a girl waiting for me at home, so for me, visiting this young Dutch woman and her kids was something simple and right. Each day, we exchanged greetings. Then after reviewing whatever food I was able to bring, I spent an hour or two on the floor with her kids, playing games.

Then, after each day's visit, I was lucky enough to do something else that made sense after all I'd been through: play jazz with a pick-up Army swing band. For the three weeks I remained in the area, we rehearsed in the afternoons, then gave dinner performances for our troops and their dates, the sweet Dutch ladies of Maastricht. Because of the necessity for total wartime blackout, 8:00 p.m. in April was the limit of our performance time. Not surprisingly, one of the hits of the day reflected the world's yearning to return to a better time.

It was titled, "When the Lights Come on Again, All over the World".

Chapter 25: Radar and Rockets

After two nights of switchboard operations, my official assignment changed for the remainder of my three total weeks in the area. I was recalled to full time duty with the 225th Anti-aircraft Searchlight Battalion which needed a radio man for a new kind of activity. I lived in a pyramidal tent by myself and was trained to do something I hadn't learned anything about in radio school: work a radar set.

Image 50: Radar Scope and Operator

Radar was still strange to me. I knew it was being used on Naval ships to detect the approach of enemy aircraft and surface subs, and I had seen it on the *Queen Elizabeth*, but I never realized it could also be used for different purposes on shore.

I worked 12-hour shifts, from a tent that was several rows of hills away from the fighting. I could see into where the Nazi positions were, but could not be seen from where I was. At this point in the war, the Nazis were all about staying back from the advancing army of the Americans, and they were launching something called V–2 rockets.

Image 51: V-2 Rocket on Meillerwagen

As rocket scientists, the Nazis were no slouches. Their V–2's were true rockets. The best of the scientists (Wernher von Braun and his rocket team) were developing Nazi missiles that were unanswerable. They took off like rockets being sent to the moon in the modern era: they started off standing on their tails belching fire directly below them, and the thrust thus generated sent them skyward on a predetermined arc in the upper stratosphere, where the low wind resistance allowed speeds of 3,500 mph.

At that speed, they traveled four to five times faster than their own noise, so there was no way they could be detected by usual means. The Nazis manufactured their V–2's in forced labor factories, but even so, there were not so many that they could launch them all day long. In addition to their speed, these rockets were extremely mobile. They could be transported anywhere, set up in very little time, and then the Nazis would shoot and scoot so as not to be detected by allied spy planes[47]. The Nazis shot the V-2s in brief salvos so that they could stretch their resources as far as possible.

Looking back on it, it's incredible how unimposing — makeshift even — some of our pivotal resources were in World War II. Within a crucial time window, I saw three scared teenagers and a baby-faced lieutenant help alter the outcome of a battle that made it into the history books — and their part was done with nothing more than the stuff they could carry on

---

[47] Spitfires were reconditioned to fly faster and farther, and then retrofitted with high resolution stereoscopic cameras to perform aerial reconnaissance missions deep into Nazi territory.

their backs. I saw a ramshackle cinder block depot dispatch men to the right time and place to matter at Buchenwald. I witnessed how the spontaneous impersonation of a superior officer had led to the sparing of lives, how garbage could keep people alive, and how one small portable switchboard connected earth-shattering American news to Holland. I saw my own life saved by: a piece of wood in the shape of a rifle stock, a tent where I was given medicine, a girls' school pressed into service as a hospital, and repeatedly, by the lowest-tech thing of all: a hole in the ground.

At this point, I suppose I shouldn't have been struck with the incongruity of high-tech radar relying on low-tech placement in a one-man tent, but I was. With the V–2, the Nazis had an indefensible weapon and they used it repeatedly on London, and later, Antwerp. But at least for warning, there were tents like mine, which not only had the radar set, but also a telephone cord that snaked out the front flap, and ultimately connected to the Air Warden Anticipation Center in London. From this modest vantage point, my job was to warn them whenever I picked up a V–2 on radar, and they would in turn would sound the sirens and allow the citizenry to get underground to safety.

Meanwhile, the US and the Nazis were in a neck-and-neck race to develop the atom bomb. If the Nazis had won, their ability to combine V–2's with nuclear warheads would surely have changed history.

When the war ended, von Braun's expertise was vied for by the Russians, who still had dreams of world conquest, and by the United States, which had no such ambitions. Fortunately, von Braun chose to bring himself, hundreds of his men, and his scientific equipment to America, where he ultimately became critically important for our space exploration program.

Image 52: Von Braun (with arm cast) immediately after his surrender

Chapter 26: Usefully Stupid

In addition to the V–2 rocket, Nazi scientists developed another unanswerable weapon: the jet airplane. The first engines were mounted in the Messerschmitt bodies, which accommodated them perfectly. We had heard about the jet, but no one had ever seen one. They traveled at 750 mph (about the speed of sound), while the best of our propeller driven fighters lumbered along at 270–300 mph, tops.

Image 53: Messerschmitt Me 262 Schwable (The World's First Jet Plane)

Safe, underground Nazi manufacturing facilities were making more than jet engines: they were pouring out completely whole jet fighters, which emerged from the underground ramps under their own power. Because of their extremely high range and speed, they could take off directly from the manufacturing plant, for deployment to any Nazi base. These jets were so protected by their speed and maneuverability that none had ever been captured intact for us to reverse engineer.

After two weeks of manning radar, the Allies captured the Mönchengladbach airport, and I was re-assigned to work with the Anti-aircraft and Searchlight crew. At the end of each runway, there was a sort of grandiose, concrete lined foxhole which contained an anti-aircraft gun and a searchlight. The muzzle of the gun and the tip of the searchlight were at about the same height as ground level, in order to keep them out of the way of potentially disabled aircraft trying to land.

Image 54: "Ready for action somewhere along the East coast of the U.S., the crew of a heavy .50-caliber antiaircraft machine gun are ready to fire as their searchlight tracks a target flying overhead." ACME News photo dated January 6, 1943

At this point, the war was winding down. We were standing in the bunker on a glorious day, when an airplane approached us with no propeller. Instead of the usual noise of a fighter-craft landing, it was at this point *gliding*, with a soft purring "swishhhhhh" [48], and we were so stupefied by the sight of an apparently engineless enemy war plane, that we forgot to shoot it down. It lowered right over our heads, giving us a worm's eye view of the plane's undercarriage. From our intimate vantage point, we could see the landing gear pistons settling into their housings. Next thing you know, we had let this swastika-emblazoned plane come in for a perfectly organized, safe landing — while our anti-aircraft gun, which we were standing right next to, remained unused.

We turned around and watched as the hatch flew open. The lone pilot's hands were up, and he stood on his seat. Pistols and rifles aimed at him were soon lowered because they realized he was unarmed and surrendering. They helped him down off of one of the wings of the plane and he walked still with hands high between them to the hangar.

Almost immediately, a crew of Army Air Corps maintenance people swarmed over the plane with brushes, painting out the swastikas on the nose and tail, and replacing them with the Stars and Stripes. Soon, the surrendering Nazi Luftwaffe lieutenant took the co-pilot's seat in the rear, while a series of American Army pilots sat in the front taking instructions[49]. One by one, American personnel were trained in the use of that jet. Most of the "students" that day were high ranking, and the highest of all was the 4-star general Hap Arnold (no relation).

When all was said and done, it was embarrassing that we had forgotten to fire, but in this case, our stupidity was far more strategic than if we'd kept our wits.

---

[48] Jets can make plenty of landing noise, as everyone knows, but the surrendering Nazi pilot had cut his engine off before we noticed him. He may have deliberately glided in, to be less likely to provoke ground fire.

[49] Until 1947, the US Air Force was a part of the US Army.

Chapter 27: Furlough to London and Paris

Hitler committed suicide on April 30, 1945, 18 days after our Buchenwald experience, Within the next eight days, Nazi units from all over surrendered to their respective opponents, formally ending the European part of World War II. In the United States, May 8 was designated as Victory in Europe Day (V-E Day)[50].

We foot soldiers were thrilled that the Allies had beaten the Nazis, but we barely had time to celebrate. Now, we had a new cloud hanging over our heads: Japan.

Japanese devotion to their emperor was total and legendary; Allied losses were expected to be upwards of a *million*. Thinking of my own plight didn't help any. Surviving frontline combat radio operators were rare, especially now, and I knew that they would never spare me. My official Walking Wounded classification would be worthless for further protection…and I couldn't stop thinking about it.

Japan.

Storming the enemy's home island while they were ready and waiting for us to jump off our landing boats — and while I was additionally freighted by the radio's 60 pounds — could only end one way for me: I would die on the shores of Japan.

While I was worrying about me, the US Army faced its own, big-time logistical challenge. It had to take stock of its troops, and re-deploy them from Europe to the Pacific. To facilitate the formidable logistics and to do so with an eye toward fairness, the Army instituted a point system. Points were assigned on the basis of, for example, how long someone had been in the service, how much of that time had been overseas, the number of months in combat, and whether someone had earned any awards. Those with especially high point totals would have the luxury of going home to America…before being sent into battle in Japan. US troops were segmented into groups with similar point totals, and to keep things wieldy, the Repple Depples were similarly segmented to serve them.

---

[50] Some parts of the world recognize May 9 as the date.

The members of our jazz group had differing point totals, so we knew that we couldn't stay together. The leader had to disband us, but as one bright spot, he let us keep our instruments. I had my high school saxophone waiting for me at home, but this one had a special meaning of its own. It was not only evocative of a chapter from *my* life, but also of someone *else's.* After the Nazi takeover, the Dutch family that owned the saxophone had wisely buried it under the dirt floor of their basement, along with the accompanying, suddenly contraband, American sheet music. Nazi occupiers might have benignly neglected the sax (or stolen it), but anything as purely American as swing-band music was strictly verboten, and any Dutch family caught with it would have faced execution. Nonetheless, when the family fell on hard times, the surviving woman of the house dug up everything, and traded both sax and music to an American GI for one safe, small luxury: a carton of cigarettes.

By the time I got it, the sax showed its adversity. The many lost or broken valve springs had been jerry-rig repaired by rubber bands. Its only "case" was a repurposed Nazi shirt sewn into a drawstring bag, which unfortunately allowed all the pieces to clank against each other, adding dents whenever it was carried. Yet, the instrument made a fine sound, and I suppose that its melodic thriving in spite of adversity was, at some level, symbolic for me.

Image 55: The Saxophone I Brought Home from the War

Because I was a relative newbie in the Army, my point total was pretty low. Purple Heart or not, there was no question about it: I would have to stay in Europe until being shipped to the front line in Japan.

Troops with about my number of total points were assigned to the Repple Depple in Munich. We knew that our time was short, and so did our commanders. We had nothing to do, and lots of anxieties to relieve, so we were given plenty of furlough time to roam the local country.

As an added diversion, some of the Repple Depples held free lottery drawings, in which a whole bunch of straws of the same length had one short straw embedded within it. In this case, drawing the short straw was a *good* thing: each holder became the winner of an especially good, longer-distance furlough. For one drawing, first prize was a trip to England. I thought, Why not enter? Maybe I'm the guy who will win. And sure enough, I was!

Better than that, I had a specific destination in mind. Earlier in the war, the Nazis had gotten as close to England as the edge of the English Channel, a mere 26 miles away. At that point, the English were making preparations for perhaps being conquered themselves. US planes were flying back and forth to London's Heathrow airport. As they were routinely arriving full and returning home empty, someone had the great idea of shuttling Jewish children to safety in America. British parents could choose to have their youngsters flown out, hopefully temporarily, where they would be safe from the advancing Nazi anti-Semitic horde. One such family had a girl of about 13 who was sent to Syracuse NY, where I was raised. In anticipation of such refugee arrivals, our rabbi asked the congregation to open its homes to the temporary adoption of Jewish children from London. Rabbi Benjamin Friedman, (our Temple's first rabbi to be born in the US) and his wife had themselves opened their home to this little girl, whose name was Mary Weingott. By now, she was already back in London. When I found out that I won the trip, I sent a letter to the last known address of Mr. and Mrs. Weingott, telling them that I would be getting a one-week furlough in London…and would they like to meet, and tell me all about what had happened back in Syracuse in the years that I was gone? They immediately responded "Yes, yes, yes, we would love to have you!"

The day came, and the lottery winners all boarded a DC3, which is what you might call a puddle jumper today.

Image 56: Douglas DC3

It was a two-engine propeller plane, and its conversion to a military aircraft was nothing fancy. All the seats were removed, and replaced with bucket seats around the perimeter. The center had been reserved for its primary payload: weapons. On that day, every one of the bucket seats was occupied by a prizewinner like me, from various replacement depots.

I had never been in an airplane before. My mother and father were frightened all their lives of flying, and did not approve of me flying at all, so this was my first time. I was all excited about it, because after what I had been through, what 19-year-old could be afraid of flying?

I boarded, and headed right for one of the seats closest to the pilots in this wide open plane. It was really fun to see all the preparations for taking off, and once airborne, pulling up the landing gear and making mid-course corrections. We flew over the beautiful sunny skies of Germany, Belgium, and France, and then ahead of us loomed the white cliffs of Dover. London was permanently bathed in fog, which for years we all thought was due to the Gulf stream winding up the shores of England, creating a difference in atmospheric pressure. Later, we learned that some of that fog was actually smog from coal dust…profuse, unending, eternal coal dust. I watched as the pilots gently lowered us by pushing forward on the twin steering gear, lower, and lower, and lower into the fog, and feeling their way down, and down — and all of a sudden in front of us loomed a huge water tower! I thought the end had come, but they both pulled back on those wheels and gunned the engines, putting us over the top with what I am sure was only a few feet to spare. They were visibly shaken; one turned to the other and said, "Well, now we know where we are!" and they made it safely into Heathrow.

When I arrived, the Weingotts had a big sign with my name on it. They rushed forward and threw their arms around me because they were so grateful for what Rabbi and Mrs. Friedman had done for their daughter, and for the wonderful friendships they had developed in Syracuse, NY.

The Weingotts *looked* like they had been through the war, and were much relieved by it being over, but Mary Weingott was a knock 'em dead beauty at age 16 or 17, and I was not used to that kind of a well-dressed, well-kept person. The German people back in Munich all looked like the elder Weingotts, having been abused by years of war.

My hosts showed me to a nice little spare bedroom, and I dropped off into the sleep usually reserved for kings and queens, between beautiful white sheets. The next morning I woke up, rubbed my eyes, and there on a hanger in my room was my Army uniform. For the first time ever, it was neatly pressed, lightly starched, and they had even found an Eisenhower type jacket that I had never owned before. In fact when I first saw people walking around in them, I thought they were butlers. I had no idea they were enlisted men wearing these gorgeous jackets. So, there was a jacket, a clean uniform, a jaunty overseas cap, and I was going to be dressed up like a human being for the first time in god knows when.

Dressed in my finery, I went downstairs to the kitchen and sat down to breakfast, just as a civilized person should. Mary said, "I am your host in London; where do you want to go?"

"Oh my gosh, where do you think I should go?"

"Well first you ought to go see Stratford-on-Avon, the home of Shakespeare. That can be our goal for the day."

Image 57: Dick Arnold in the Eisenhower Jacket 1946

The village was delightful, my guide was well informed, and she was lovely to behold. Each of the furlough's seven days was a similar success. We saw the Tower of London, and took the marvelous rail accommodations all over the place, enjoying each other's company. She knew my sweetheart back home and though there was no romantic attachment between Mary and me — it certainly was delightful.

At the end of the seventh day, they took me to the depot, we tearfully bade goodbye, and I returned to the US Army airbase at Heathrow. I tried not to think about Japan, but whenever I slowed down, I could feel it looming.

Thankfully, the next day offered a new distraction. The weather was socked-in solid, and no planes could fly, so they told us to take an extra day off. As it turns out, the bad weather continued, turning that extra day into an extra seven.

Finally they decided to ship us back to mainland Europe on a boat, and from there to Paris on the train. We needed to get back to our Repple Depple in Munich, and the two railroad stations in Paris, North and South Stations, were connected by a long subway ride. The problem is that I really didn't know how to get from one to the other (smile, smile, smile), and since I was "hopelessly lost", it took me *another* seven days to find my way to South Station. (Never did tell anybody that I knew how to speak French.)

I was on my own in Paris, and the very first place I headed for was the Louvre. We had studied this famous national art museum at great length in military prep school. I arrived at the door and was met by a guard. He was totally impressed by my gorgeous full dress uniform with that Eisenhower jacket and jaunty overseas cap Everything was clean and pressed and spotless and he was sure that I must have been some kind of officer. He said "Normally zee museum because of wartime situation is not open to members d'autres armed forces, but obviously you are a person of some integrity and if you want a veezeet, you can."

So thanks to the thoughtfulness of the Weingotts and this man, I was one of the few privileged outsiders to visit the Louvre at the time. I had never thought about it before, but war was hard on museums, too. Fuel was strictly rationed, including for the occupying Nazis, so statues and other indestructibles were relegated to the unheated reaches of the museum. Even *Winged Victory,* dating from nearly 200 BC, was considered safe enough in an unheated section of the building. But because extremes of temperature were sure to wreck oil paintings, the museum's many precious originals were all temporarily located in one huge central pavilion that still had some heat. The paintings of the Louvre had to be densely packed to fit into the heated portion of the museum, so they were all gathered into racks, sort of like books resting on their bindings, and with their pages leafing upward. Some of the pictures were huge, and you could look at them one by one by turning the leaves. I was delighted by being able to do just that, handling every one of those gorgeous priceless paintings.

I remember realizing that my fingerprints were all over the frame of the *Mona Lisa,* and if she ever got stolen, I would be a prime suspect!

Image 58: The Mona Lisa

Chapter 28: Furlough to Mt. Blanc

In August 1945, I won the lottery again.

This time we got on a train in Munich and headed for the Mountain Paradise of Chamonix, France[51]. Chamonix was a border city at the base of Mt. Blanc, the tallest mountain in the Alps (about three miles high). The tip of Mt. Blanc is where the borders of Italy, France, and Switzerland meet. At that time there was what they call a cog railway. Because of the steep grade, there was a third rail in the center, which meshed with cogs underneath the engine and cars, to keep them from slipping downhill. The engine and its boiler had to be tipped, too, so as to be more or less level while on the mountain's incline.

Image 59: Cog Railway in Shneeberg

---

[51] French pronunciation: "sham-o-NEE".

Unlike many of the climbing trains today, this one went up the side of Mt. Blanc in a circular path, so that as it circled the tip of the mountain it would progressively pass through Switzerland, Italy, and France — and as the tip narrowed, it would "travel" more and more frequently from one country to the next, till all three met at the top. Mt. Blanc has perpetual snow, so we would stop and view the scenery at various places and have snowball fights, which was especially fun in August. Then, too, because of the vertical drop at the peak of Mt. Blanc, if you pitched a snowball straight out into space it would go a long, long way. We took lots of pictures.

Many years later, my granddaughter Tosca wrote to ask me, "Grandpa have you ever been to Italy?" Italy is the home of half her ancestry, and because she was preparing for her first trip, she wanted some tips on what to do and see.

"Yes, Tosca, I have been to Italy four times."

"Oh, I bet you know a lot!"

"Well, not really…you see it was four different times in the same day!" and I explained to her about the cog railroad.

After journeying to the tip of Mt. Blanc and back down, we settled into a beautiful resort hotel in Chamonix, where we were delighted to find that the meals were simply exquisite.

"Wait a minute", we said to each other. "Where did all this great food come from in a world that has just been through a devastating war?" It turned out that this was American GI rations prepared by one of the most famous chefs in the world. He had taken the same ingredients of what usually wound up as slop thrown onto our mess gear, and made beautiful creations worthy of gracing the tables of the Waldorf Astoria in New York.

But after our joyride to the top of Mt. Blanc, something more important than good food awaited us.

On August 6th, the United States had dropped its first atomic bomb on Hiroshima. Everybody at the hotel was agog with the news, but we didn't know what the Sam Hill they were talking about. "What do you mean 'atomic bomb'? What's an atomic bomb?" Its development had been a well-kept secret, so nobody knew very much. But now, the media's analysis was that maybe things were gonna be a lot different for us in Japan.

I would have hated President Truman's job when it was time to decide whether to drop the world's first atom bomb. But if he hadn't done so, I would have hated *my* job. On August 9th, we were still in France when President Truman ordered the second atomic bombing of the Allies' only remaining enemy. By August 15th, their official surrender signaled that World War II was finally over. It was now a sure fact that we would never have to face the formidable Japanese defense of their emperor.

If I ever went to Japan, it wouldn't be to die on its sandy shores, after all.

Image 60: The Atomic Bombing of Nagasaki

Chapter 29: Hitler's Lightbulb

So, World War II was over, and there we were, having made it back to our Repple Depple in Munich, Germany. But it would still be awhile before I could go home. Remember, those with high point totals got first priority. Imagine a couple of million men trying to get home all at once; it was going to take time. Again, we were given unlimited furloughs. Those who never returned from furloughs on time didn't get any more, but in this, I was a good boy, and they even bought into the story that I had been lost for seven days in Paris. I was given furloughs as I wished. Since the other two had been in London and France / Italy / Switzerland, this time I wanted to see what was going on around me.

The trip that stands out most in my mind was a visit to Hitler's Eagle's Nest, which was at the conjoining boundary lines of Germany, Austria, and Czechoslovakia.

Image 61: The Eagle's Nest

After Austria, the Sudetenland portion of Czechoslovakia was the next of the European countries to fall under the Nazi Regime. Hitler had walked into there claiming that its people were German Nationals. It had belonged to Germany before it was taken from them in WWI, and therefore he felt justified in taking it back. This of course, was one of the ultimate tests of the West's resolve to confront Hitler. Chamberlain was the Prime Minister of England, and he signed a treaty with Hitler, saying OK, you can have this part of Czechoslovakia, if you promise to be a good boy and not invade anything else. Hitler signed the treaty and subsequently broke it by annexing other parts of Czechoslovakia. But all that was history and I wanted to see the Nest from where Hitler conducted some of his vicious war. Presumably, this spot had been picked for two reasons: the overriding beauty of its Alpine heights, and because he could look out over his Germany and native land of Austria, as well as other conquered lands.

This Eagle's Nest was perched on the top of his mountain, and in order to get to it, you drove up a road that wound around the mountain for about a quarter of the way, where it ended in a big parking lot carved into the rock face. From there, a beautifully ornamented, concrete-walled tunnel with soft lighting took you to the center of the mountain, ending at an elevator such as no one had ever had seen before.

Image 62: The Eagle's Nest Tunnel

Image 63: Elevator Entrance

Although it is now a single-car with no benches, it was then a triple-decker elevator, with the middle one especially posh. They explained to us that Hitler's guards would first enter the top car, which then rose to allow Hitler and any visiting big shots to enter the middle one. Finally, more guards entered the lowest car, so that Hitler was vertically surrounded by protection. Really neat. The center car was plush, plush, plush…better than anything I had seen in the high-rises of New York. It was roomy and well lit. In fact, there were lamps all around the inside. And inside the lamps were bulbs unlike anything I had seen before. They were elongated, oval-shaped, and clear so that you could see the filaments inside them. Beautiful, sparkling light bulbs.

Image 64: The Eagle's Nest Elevator

For the trip up, I was the only one in the elevator, and I thought, this is my chance for a souvenir to send home. I reached up and, as if extracting an auto lamp, gave it a twist and pulled it straight out. I stole it and hid it in my pocket and didn't feel the least bit guilty. When I got to the top I saw the most gorgeous view through a gargantuan plate glass window overlooking Hitler's Empire (and no doubt feeding his ego).

The trip down was uneventful. I wasn't the only one in the elevator now, but nobody detected my stolen lamp bulb.

When I got back to my Repple Depple, I went where no one could see that I had stolen an artifact of der wonderful stinkin' Fuhrer, and I packed it very very carefully with all kinds of cotton, wool, and anything else I could find. I didn't quit till it was packed, boxed, and taped beautifully, and I passed it through the export facility at the Repple Depple without any question and sent it home addressed to my mother and father.

Much later, when I got home, my mother mentioned receiving the package, but since the bulb didn't fit any of the sockets in our house, she threw it away!

Chapter 30: The Trip Home

As I had a very low points total in the priority for rotating troops home, my time to go back to civilization wasn't until late December of 1945 — four months after World War II was over with Japan, and seven months after it was over in Europe.

So far, I had been to England twice during the War. First, shortly after we arrived on the *Queen Elizabeth,* and second, for my furlough with Mary Weingott and her family. This, my third time, was finally to prepare for going home. We went by truck and it was the happiest moment of my life, because I was going home and the War was over! It was a long and arduous trip, but not one complaint from the whole gang. When we got to Le Havre, France, I marveled at how well the port had already been restored. From there, we ferried the 26 miles to Dover, England, complete with fog. Once in London, I learned that there was an arrangement for American troops to call home. Remember that there were no cell phones or satellites in those days, and calling back to the States relied on a huge, long cable laid under the ocean. One of the very few transoceanic cable links was dedicated to those American soldiers who wanted to call home, and its access all originated from a single phone booth in Trafalgar Square[52]. The phone booth was near the base of Lord Nelson's statue and there was a huge long line snaking around the park, across the road, and back on the other side. It looked hopeless for anyone to reach the front of it, but the motivation was magnetic. The line was shortest at night, and since this took place in December in foggy snowy wet England, it was cold. Having lived through freeze-burn injuries that put me in the hospital for three months, it was terrible pain, but the call home was going to be worth it. I think I put on every garment I owned. All night long I kept edging forward. We were limited to two minutes each, scrupulously governed by Military Police who made sure that at two minutes, you hung up. Finally I made it to the front row. Because of the time zone differences between London and Syracuse, my mother was at home and my father at work.

"Mom, Mom, it's me!!" I joyfully shouted.

---

[52] Trafalgar Square is a famous landmark in central London commemorating the Battle of Trafalgar in 1805.

And she said "Oh…" kind of nonchalantly for our first conversation since I had been at war. And then flatly, "How are you doing?"

"Fine, fine, fine. I am getting ready to come home!"

"Oh… That's good," again nonchalantly.

I was kind of surprised at her total lack of affect, but she finally became fluent enough to bring me up to date on my sisters Lois and Dorothy, and their husbands and children, and my aunts and uncles (which were many, because we came from big families). We had a good thing going, though she refused to discuss my girlfriend, who was one of the main reasons I wanted to get home. At least that part was normal; I expected it: I was deeply in love with my sweetheart, but my parents weren't.

When our two minutes were up, it all seemed like a second to me.

"Goodbye," she said.

"I can't wait to see you!"

"Goodbye," she said again.

Then the MP hung up the receiver.

When it was time for my group of soldiers to go home, we boarded a Liberty Ship. Liberty Ships were the smallest ocean going vessels used regularly in WWII. They were built on an automobile production line to maximize delivery. The ships were the largest that could be made this way, but they were very small for ocean-going vessels[53]. They had a cargo hold designed as a wide open space, and that's all there was. The bottom part of the cargo hold was used as a food service, and that's where we ate, cafeteria style. From the bottom of the hull right straight up to the deck, that whole open cargo space was now filled with hammocks strung from pole to pole, and you climbed up ladders depending on which bunk was yours. When you were lying in the bunk face up, your nose was practically touching the bottom of the hammock above you. If there was such a thing as claustrophobia, this is where you got it.

---

[53] The US Merchant Marine website reports that Liberty Ship engines generated 2500 horsepower, and a speed of 11 knots. Nicknamed "ugly ducklings" by President Franklin Delano Roosevelt, they were designed for emergency construction http://www.usmm.org/libertyships.html. In comparison, the *RMS Queen Elizabeth* generated 160,000 hp and 29 knots, even though it was probably 12 times heavier at over 83,000 tons. http://ww2ships.com/acrobat/us-os-001-f-r00.pdf.

What a difference between the deluxe, stately *RMS Queen Elizabeth* that took us to war over unusually calm seas, and traveling back home now.

Image 65: Liberty Ship at Sea

For haste, Liberty Ships were production-line welded, not put together with rivets. That meant that there was no give at all. There was a penalty to this inflexibility which was compounded by their flat-bottomed design: as the ship ploughed forward, the incoming waves (driven predominantly by western winds) would hit the prow square on and raise it straight up, levering the stern under water, during which time the propeller drove the ship. But when the stern levered out of the water, the propeller spun pointlessly in the air, making a horrible "whappity, whappity, whappity, whappity, whap" before hammering back down with a "Slam!…Wham!" At first, we all had headaches from the racket, but finally, we got to the point where we were simply miserable and didn't know one headache from the next.

It was January, and the North Atlantic served up 14 different, unnamed storms in the 16 days that it took us to cross. When you went down to the cafeteria at the bottom to have your meals, if the weather was rough, you immediately lost whatever you had eaten, and it was really a mess. The only way that you can avoid vomiting over and over in a space that has no portal or view of the outdoors is to get up on deck if you can. Imagine the deck, with its cables running from bow to stern, so that you could grab onto one of them to keep from being thrown overboard. At least, when you are above decks, you can see the waves coming, and adjust your body to a shock that you can anticipate. Up and down, with water thrown right over your head directed by the ship's prow.

The first time I caught on to the idea of standing by the prow so as not to throw up, I looked up as a wave broke over me and there, right over my head, was what I thought was a shark! I now think it was probably a dolphin, because they have the habit of swimming alongside of ships' prows, while sharks do not. But to my untrained eye, it was a shark. Whether friendly mammal or potential predator, watching either was better than staying below and throwing up. Anyway, most of us had probably been through much worse. At this point, anything survivable was OK with us. We were going home again!

When we finally cruised into the New York harbor and passed the Statue of Liberty in the calm Hudson River, we knew that we had made it home for real. Sadly, though, we heard that two of the Liberty Ships lost their rudders in one or another of those nameless storms. No one told us more, but a rudderless, small, rigid Liberty Ship probably couldn't have survived without the ability to keep its nose pointed into the huge waves.

We boarded Army buses, and crossed the George Washington Bridge into New Jersey. We were back at Fort Dix, which is where I started my Army service as a *much* younger man 16 months earlier. They had us turn in our rifles (yes, we had dragged them with us on the trip home). When I handed mine over to the supply sergeant, I vowed that I would never, ever pick up a firearm again. I had seen what they could do to human beings and by interpolation, thought about what they would do to animals, and certainly what they would do in the hands of the wrong people. So, no hunting for me. No shooting galleries, even. A few years later, I would love taking my kids to amusement parks, and they could all shoot if they wanted, but I never did.

There was a card table at the exit of Fort Dix, and sitting there were two recruiters for the National Guard.

"Soldier, why not sign up for the National Guard and earn a living while you are helping protect our country?"

"No…thanks."

"But wait, you can keep your present rank!" Oh my god, I thought. Private First Class. Thank you, but no thank you.

The first optional thing I did after arriving at Fort Dix was to call Mom and Dad. My travel plans were simple. I was going to get on the train at Grand Central station, and make whatever connections I needed to. One way or another, I would be home in a couple of days.

When I got them on the phone, my father was ecstatic, but my mother was again surprisingly laid back. They both met me at the station in Syracuse, and drove me home. I immediately bounded upstairs with my saxophone over my shoulder in its cloth bag. I opened the door and stepped into my room.

There was no bed!

My furniture was gone, too. My pictures on the wall, gone…my banners from Syracuse, MIT, Manlius Military, Nottingham High…all of them…gone! Even my Boy Scout knot-board that had earned me a Merit Badge… gone! There were no drawers to open, but I did go to the closet. It was stripped clean, except for one, overlooked item in the way back on a shelf: my clarinet, thank the good lord! It was in a black box in a black closet and high up; evidently whoever had stolen everything from my room had at least missed this beautiful clarinet made of Mexican granadilla wood.

"MOM! DAD! What happened to my room, my furniture, my banners! Where are they?"

And my mother said, "I gave them all away."

"What…you gave them all away?"

"Yes. You were dead, and I gave them all away."

"Dead? I never died!"

"Well, as far as I was concerned, at the time you did — because the postman delivered all of your belongings and that is only done for people who have been killed in the war."

"Mom, I am here…here I am! I called you from Fort Dix. I called you from London, for crying out loud. And I'm sure that Rabbi Hyman told you that he had seen me, and that I was OK…"

Later that day, my father recreated for me the scene in which I had died.

"One day, the postman rang the doorbell, and while I was standing by, he handed your mother a package — a cellophane wrapped package that had your clothes and your personal belongings all respectfully and neatly folded, with your now empty barracks bag also folded and placed on top. He bowed, and said quietly, 'These are the belongings of your son, Richard.' Your Mom said, 'Oh, my God. He's dead. Dick is dead.'

"I wondered about whether you were really dead, because I never got a telegram from the War Department. And when you called from London, I knew you were OK. You wrote continuously, and I showed your Mom, but I could not convince her that you weren't dead.

"And even now, I don't think she believes that you are alive."

Chapter 31: America after the War

World War II was exhausting for the people at home. For four years, they had grieved over the loss of their young men overseas, worried about their youngest children's futures, and suffered over whether America would continue to exist as a free entity.

The communication lag of those days could lead to ironies so terrible that they are barely comprehensible today: the postman might deliver a son's last optimistic letter for his parents to read — days after they had already received official notice of his death.

Understandably then, when all of this was finally over, elation at home was total.

Image 66: Victory in Japan Day celebration at Times Square August 14, 1945[54]

---

[54] For me, this photo of elated Americans is evocative of the moment I learned I would not have to die in Japan. But just to be clear, celebrating your own survival is not the same as celebrating the mass death of any country's civilians. I find no joy in that at all.

Against this backdrop, a soldier returning from the front lines — often many months after the news of the War's end — came home to find that everyone else had moved on. In the country's eagerness to look forward, even loving siblings and parents only wanted to know so much about the past. As a result, the surviving frontline GI had no one to talk to about what he had seen, endured…and inflicted. This too, was consonant with the times. After all, in the 1940's, America was far from ready to talk openly about some of life's biggest ideas like sex, pregnancy and labor, and death. And it would be years before mental illness could be talked about in polite company. Indeed, Posttraumatic Stress Disorder (PTSD) wasn't added to the official manual of the American Psychiatric Association until 1980.

WWII was perceived by most Americans as a just war that our country did not start, and in that sense, its returning soldiers were lucky. But though we were received generally as heroes, in those days we could not be received as what we were most particularly: individuals with invisible pains as real as those that were visible. In light of my own experience returning home, I have often considered how much more terrible it was for our returning Vietnam veterans 25-30 years later: though carrying the same burdens, they were denied a hero's welcome.

The survivors are victims, too. For me, just seeing Buchenwald made me a victim, and in my mother's case, even *mistakenly* thinking that I was dead led to her own post-traumatic stress disorder. Yet, PTSD cannot be the last summary of one's life.

In my case, I was privileged to live. And that meant I could set about keeping The Pledge made at Buchenwald.

Afterword: The Pledge as a Work in Progress

For a short while after the War, Dick was back in Boston. While there, he started an informal basketball league for the 9 and 10 year-old kids of hard-working families living in the impoverished areas by the docks. He couldn't stay at MIT for long, though: he found he was no longer able to excel at math and formula memorization. Also, it was too hard to be separated from Franny, the sweetheart who had sustained him while he was at war. They had had only one date before he left, but their letters grew increasingly impassioned, and they fell deeply in love. For a while, he hitchhiked home every weekend to be with her, but soon, they eloped, settled into an apartment, and were husband and wife as fellow undergraduates at Syracuse University.

As a result of his upbringing, combined with his experiences as a soldier, he was by then both a Christian and a Jew. After moving back to Syracuse, he told his rabbi about The Pledge, as a way to be "on call" for something potentially useful. One of the members of the temple, Judge Abelson, had been hearing strange reports about the staff of a local detention home abusing its kids. The counselors were said to be systematically spraying them with high-pressure water hoses, in order to intimidate them into joining their crime gang. The stories were so fantastic that verification was in order, before launching a formal investigation. The Judge sent Dick to the detention home with a credible reason to be there: he was a young man who had recently been in the service, and as part of an enrichment program, would be teaching kids the principles of freedom. Stunningly, the rumors turned out to be true, and the Judge saw that those responsible were arrested and jailed.

In 1968, at the height of America's protests over racism, sexism, and the Vietnam War, Dick got a call from his oldest son Marc, then a sophomore at Columbia.

"Dad, you're going to hate me for this. I've been arrested. I'm in jail."

Marc had been involved in a sit-in that took over the University president's office, protesting what the students interpreted as a segregationist move by the University: building (within a city-owned park) a gymnasium designed with two separate entrances and facilities —

one for University members, and one for the local residents of Harlem[55]. Dick saw his son as carrying on a family value — fighting for his belief in how others should be treated — and responded accordingly: "Marc, I don't hate you for it…I *love* you for it!"

Some years later, managing his own marketing business, Dick was rushing to a sales meeting in New York City's Times Square. As he emerged from the cab, striding to the building with briefcase in hand, a young man in his 20's tapped him on the shoulder and asked, "What have you done for God lately?"

Normally, even Dick might have dismissed this person as a big-city nut. But, it was April, and all that day, he had been deep in thought about Buchenwald, and what he and the other soldiers had promised each other. Dick realized he hadn't been working his pledge any time recently, and had been brooding about it. The truth being inescapable, he took a moment to process this stranger's question, and answered it honestly:

"Nothing. I don't know who you are, but you have asked the right question on the right day. If you come back at six o'clock this evening, I'll be here to talk."

No wonder Buchenwald had been on Dick's mind: that day was its 30th anniversary.

At their meeting, the stranger said, "I'm with a missionary church. Frankly, we don't ever approach people your age, but something just lead me to do it. God said to me, 'Touch this man.'"

Dick studied with the church for a year, and then embarked on an initiative with 14 of his younger classmates. At that time, one of the old Newark prisons had been reactivated to accommodate the swelling ranks of the poor black inhabitants who were arrested for protesting the miserable living conditions in their white-owned tenements. The crumbling prison was in a poor part of town, located across the street from an abandoned strip mall.

Dick and his team walked into the prison, and asked how they could be of service. The Warden spoke with directness.

---

[55] See http://www.columbia.edu/cu/computinghistory/1968.

"Christians, you say. You should know what you're getting into: this prison holds 500 men and 50 women who are almost 100% black Muslims. So if you want to talk to them about Christianity, I don't think that you'll have much of a chance."

"No, we're not here to proselytize, we're here on a mission to help people in trouble."

The Warden laid out his plan, which he never thought would get beyond the aspiration stage. The maximum term in his facility was 18 months, and the way he saw it, most of the people there were basically not criminals. They were people protesting segregation and the unfair conditions that kept them impoverished. His idea was to have a Work Release program: qualified prisoners would get a job on the outside while they were still in prison. As he envisioned it, for five mornings a week, an unmarked van would take them to their work, where only the heads of the companies that hired them would know their situation. At the end of the day, the same unmarked van would take them back to stay overnight in the prison.

But then, he explained his own Catch-22[56] situation. "The problem with my plan is that they cannot apply for a job while they are in prison…and they can only go out for Work Release if they already have a job."

If they could ever break that cycle, he knew what he would do next: administer an aptitude test to his Work Release candidates, to see what they might be suited for. With that documentation, someone could go out into the community to talk with prospective employers. Given the racial tensions of the times, it would have to be blacks employing blacks.

In contrast to his vision, the Warden summed up reality: "When someone has completed their term here, we hand them five dollars, the clothes they were wearing when they came in, give them a pat on the back, and wish them Good Luck. What can you do with five dollars, a suit of dirty clothes, and a prison record?"

The Warden advised Dick how they could help. "Across the street is a strip mall where all the stores are empty. Somehow, raise the money to rent a storefront, equip it with cots and food. Then those who are released would have a place to stay. They could work, practice their religion as they see fit, and finally have a chance at life."

---

[56] The term Catch-22 was coined by Joseph Heller in his novel of that name. It refers to any frustrating situation in which one is trapped by contradictory regulations or conditions.(See http://dictionary.reference.com/browse/catch-22)

With admiration for the Warden (who had risen through the ranks as a policeman in that neighborhood), Dick wrote a grant application to Rutgers University. The reviewers responded positively on one condition: the missionaries come up with matching funds. They did so, through the unlikely source of the 4-H Club. Even though that organization was about kids, and not inner-city adults, someone working with them came through.

When Dick realized he could no longer tolerate the Northeast winters (cold reawakened the pain in his wartime freeze injuries), he and his current wife Beth moved to North Carolina. Having a Master's degree in counseling, Beth landed a job in a Group Home, which provided a place for in-trouble kids to avoid detention homes. In most of the cases, the child's problem was traceable to a dysfunctional parental relationship. They realized that in order to provide a meaningful way out for these kids, they themselves would need specialized training. They studied Family Therapy counseling, which involved going into the home to see a family's dynamics firsthand. In this model, the counselors have to be husband and wife, though only one of them needs to be formally certified. Beth already was, which allowed them to serve as a team.

After running the Group Home, Beth took on responsibilities at a Safe Home for battered women. Through Beth's on-the-job exposure there, they realized that because no one was working with the batterers, it was pointless to hope for meaningful change. They came to the unorthodox conclusion that that batterers needed attention, too, which was a role that Dick took on. For both Beth and Dick, this was an intense time: rewarding work, but not sustainable forever.

By their mid-50's, they owned their first motor home and sold advertising space in a real estate magazine partially adaptable to local markets. One of the businessmen that Dick approached was Guy Hill, founder of Hill Aircraft, located at a county airport outside of Atlanta. His primary customers were CEO's. Guy sold and serviced their corporate aircraft, and trained their pilots to fly them. He knew his customers well, and they trusted him.

Guy was not interested in Dick's sales pitch, but he had read the book that Dick published as a result of his and Beth's experiences in family centered therapy[57]. In it, he saw something of Dick's earnestness, and called back with a counterproposal.

---

[57] *How to Solve Everyday Problems ... With God's Help.*

As a successful businessman, Guy had been thinking about how to give back to the community, and was convinced that other CEO's would also respond to the opportunity to do something personally meaningful. He outlined his idea for a CEO Executive Forum, which was to be a low-profile think-tank: no dues, no fancy letterheads, no fund-raising, no media posturing, no politicians. Their first charge was to settle on one community problem that governmental agencies could not handle. Their second charge as volunteers was to conceive an approach that could be totally handled by additional volunteer resources.

Image 67: CEO Executive Forum Publication 1988 with Guy Hill

The Executive Forum included 25 Atlanta-based business leaders selected by Guy. Dick served as Executive Director, and the Forum met for 6:00 a.m. breakfasts around a huge circular conference table, once a month for two years. All activities on everyone's part were on a volunteer basis. Dick and Beth stretched their resources to stick with it.

The Forum relaxed its stipulation of restricting themselves to one problem when they realized that two of those on their final list were highly interrelated: bullying and the use of addictive drugs among school children. With the help of volunteer expert lecturers such as respected educationalist Albert Shanker[58], they came to see these problems as two sides of the same coin: the end-purpose of both is to enslave.

By this time (1986-87), Atlanta's Superintendent of Schools had already implemented an important milestone on his own: he made sure that inner city Project kids were bused to Harwell, one of the black K-5 schools in a better neighborhood. In the midst of a still overtly-segregated society, his motive was simple: let the poorer children see for themselves that an alternative future was within their grasp. The Superintendent and the school's Principal agreed that Harwell was ideally suited to explore the Forum-created after-school concept. First, test the impact of an after-school program for providing support on traditional subjects. Later, they would tackle the additional challenges inherent in substance abuse and bullying.

Permission notices were sent home with the kids bused in from the Projects, and most of the parents were thrilled at the prospect of a solid after-school opportunity. Beth became the After-School Director and Curriculum Administrator.

As per The Forum's plan, nearby high school seniors got involved. Already obligated to perform community service before graduation, a senior could go to Harwell after school and mentor several youngsters. The seniors assisted their charges in understanding the homework for the school day just ended. The kids were able to do their homework quickly, do it right, and to be certified by their mentor as getting it right.

The youngest children were each given a dollar to spend at a local five-and-dime store. Any time a kid correctly figured out how much change to expect from the transaction, s/he got to keep both the item and the change.

---

[58]Former president of the American Federation of Teachers http://www.shankerinstitute.org/about.

When a 3rd-grade teacher asked for help engaging her pupils, they tried something more abstract: a points-reward system. They allotted a certain number points for showing up on time, and so many for doing their homework right. Accumulated points were converted into a cash reward in the form of a check. About every two months, the teachers walked the kids to a bank, where they could learn firsthand about the process of cashing their checks. With earned cash now in hand, the kids went to the county airport, where they could shop at a hangar that had been set up with an array of candy, basketballs, baseballs, dolls, flowers, etc. — all donated by local merchants[59]. The two children with the highest points were treated to plane rides, sitting right up next to the pilot.

At that time, early computer games were taking hold of the commercial-grade marketplace. Vendors were phasing out their obsolescent pin-ball machines, and beginning to fill their warehouses with them. Dick went to a major supplier, and explained their idea for putting the old machines to work as an instant reward for inner-city kids who aced each day's homework (with a mentoring Senior who certified it). Dick remembers almost having to jump out of the way as they loaded trucks with pin-ball machines, gave him bags full of the slugs that their mechanics carried with them for making repairs in the field, and wished the CEO's God-speed in their program to help inner-city kids.

Soon, children who had always avoided eye contact with their teachers were waving their hands in the air to be called on. Grades went up. In succeeding weeks, the children needed less and less academic mentoring from the seniors, though they continued to thrive on their attention.

This kind of work, obviously driven by good spirit, has a way of bringing out the best in others: one of the CEO's was from Arby's, which donated lunch for the Saturday kids program; several off-duty policemen volunteered their time during school hours; the bank that cashed the 3rd-graders' checks wouldn't accept reimbursement from the teachers. And the most commonly selected item by those hard-working 3rd-grade shoppers at the hangar mart? Something for their mothers.

In his 87th year, Dick is working on the next-generation of the after-school program: adding an anti-drug / anti-bullying component to the scholastic subjects. High school seniors

---

[59] This was at Fulton County Airport, the location of Hill Aircraft. Executive Forum CEO's were among the local merchants making the donations.

will work with 4th-graders, who are at the right intersection of being old enough to teach…and young enough to reach.

A Nephew's Perspective

As a kid, I didn't know what to make of the author. Just that he was an uncle, and different from the other grown-ups around me: the complete unselfconsciousness of his cheerful enthusiasm struck me as being more like that of a slightly older kid from camp than that of an adult. Because I didn't understand this, I always felt, well…a little uncomfortable.

When I was little and my mother was still alive, we saw him fairly often. After she was gone, I occasionally overheard bits of news: "Well, for a couple of years, he was helping detention-home kids; now he's working with prisoners on job placement." I didn't see the theme in any of this, and as I was busy with my own life, I let these fragments remain fragments.

Then, last year, after at least 30 years of having been out of touch with each other, I was surprised to receive an e-mail from him, inviting me to his birthday party in Georgia.

Georgia?

I didn't even know I *had* relatives living in Georgia! My first reaction was a moment of the old discomfort. But then I figured, *What does a man have to do besides live to be 85…and ask?* So, I went.

My sisters and I drove for two hours from the nearest airport, and discovered that while rent-a-car navigators are good enough for *finding* a trailer park, they're worthless at finding a specific location *within* it. (Appreciating the irony of our difficulty in finding the author's house — with a satellite navigator, in perfect weather, in broad daylight — would have to wait until my plane ride home.)

All unspoken anxiety and anticipation, we knocked. We were warmly received as we squeezed through the entryway, past the breakfast nook, and into the living room. Looking through a picture window, I could see the lake that no doubt accounted for why he and Beth had settled here more than 20 years ago. Projecting out over the water is a beckoning deck that he built when he was 65.

The conversation was instantly warm, but after a while, I noticed that something on the wall was distracting me. I'm afraid I progressively seceded from the conversation, abandoning my sisters to handle a decent chunk of the past several decades on their own.

What *is* that thing on the wall?

I'm too far away to figure it out, and for some reason, too stubborn to cheat by simply approaching it. Something in a small glassed-in frame. Finally, I give up all pretense of conversation, and move in for a closer look. So *that's* what a Purple Heart is.

How'd I get to be an adult without knowing that my Mom's brother was wounded in World War II? Perhaps I was too young for her to talk to about such things before she died. But *he* is still here, and could tell me about it for himself. I asked.

On the plane ride heading home, I was transfixed by the writings he gave me. The author is not very well summed up by being the uncle I didn't understand. If succinctness is in order, here's a better summary: he's one of the people to thank for our freedom.

In helping him to prepare this book from the many drafts of his experiences, I was treated to a number of firsts. I met my fine relative Guido (the author's grandson) for the first time and became part of their pre-existing team, adding my generation as a third in between theirs. I learned how devastated my grandmother was by the mistaken conclusion that her son had died as a solider. Hearing the strangeness of her reaction was particularly startling to me, since I knew and enjoyed her as a woman of pioneer stock: incisive, resolute, confident, opinionated even, yet gifted with warmth and humor. I loved hearing what a fine older sister my Mom always was to the author, how all three kids harmonized together, and especially the stories of sibling conspiracy to put one over on their parents.

Finally, I discovered that the theme to my uncle's various enterprises (previously so elusive to me as to seem scattershot) is not only clear, but irrepressibly so. I am no longer a little uncomfortable. What I am is proud. He has chosen to invest the expense of his unspeakable experiences as a 19-year-old foot soldier into the drive to foster better human understanding. It is that drive that has impelled the author for 66 years, and counting.

                                                                                Frederick Gale, MD
                                                                                 October 26, 2011

For Dad, Who Just Celebrated His 86th Birthday

No one wants to wake up before dawn, of course. Certainly not during summer when days are long and evenings linger. But early Saturday mornings, when my chance as the third of six children finally came around, Dad awakened me with gentle singing.

Never mind that the sky was dark with only the faintest touch of orangey pink. It would soon transform into vibrancy. This was our day to go fishing. I knew no better delight than squirming into inelegant clothing, journeying in our cumbersome family car on an empty road and later coming home with the scent of summer.

My Dad was more perfect than anyone's. He was the father who cut off pumpkin tops and, letting us scrape out the innards, baked creamy pumpkin pies from scratch; knew all the lyrics to hundreds of songs, taught us the thrills of harmonizing and rapid tongue-twisters; was a grassroots researcher, self-taught in the obscure details of myriad topics; an animated storyteller always good for spinning a yarn; and an ingenious mister-fix-it, natural-born to repair the irreparable.

At age seven or eight, I couldn't have known my father's hidden pain, his retained images from The War. We hadn't yet been told how Dad had nearly frozen to death in a foxhole between two friends who actually had; how he'd subsequently spent three months in a French hospital growing his skin back. How a sheltered 19 year-old, the Jewish high school graduate of an elite military academy — under the impression that he'd never see combat — became inextricably involved in the front line. Eventually, with a treasured Purple Heart medal and a mind filled with tragic memories, Dad came home like so many World War II veterans, with no link between the idealized post-war world and that horrific conglomeration of memories which shattered his youthful innocence.

I was the oldest girl of my father's six children. My two elder brothers, Marc and Joe, were naturally expected to fish alongside Dad. So, too, was our younger brother, Marty, the twin of Mimi. She and Wendy, like me, figured equally into our father's Upstate New York fishing schedule. But because I was older than my sisters, they had to wait out those years when dangerous waters and sleeping schedules prevented them from fishing. My enthusiasm surprised and pleased my father, as I was otherwise interested in girlish things like ballet. At any rate, the six of us children growing up in Dad's household had no awareness of Dad's life as a soldier. We did see a few photos of a young man in uniform, and in Sunday school we heard about the Holocaust, but otherwise there wasn't an avenue for connecting our Dad with warfare.

Love for my father and love for the quiet scenery we inhabited were equal motivators for my joining him as a fishing companion. We each found comfort and uplift in the complexities and richness of our idyllic fishing sites. We meandered in quietude, abstractly pondering the most likely spot for fish to gather. We paused in mid-step and felt no sense of urgency. We noted passing birds and flitting water bugs. We laughed at frogs. We watched the sky brighten. We took it all in as two complementary parts of an ever-changing yet dependable and interdependent environment.

Dad's excitement at my inadvertently snagging a fish was always with kindly, calm praise as we collaboratively pulled those lovely, slippery rainbow trout with their shimmery, multi-colored speckled bodies, up from the morning's shining waters. Their beauty and vitality elicited profound awe in me. Yet within a split-second I'd instinctively pull back, horrified. Those poor fish thrashed crazily at the double shock of being extracted from the water's life-force while at the same time fighting futilely against the long, spear-like curve of a hook which cut more profoundly through the lip at each yank. How cruel of us to trick those fish with fake flies attached to sharpened metal! I shuddered to think that those wondrous imitation flies, colorfully tied little works of art which my father had handcrafted himself, were the source of such twisting desperation.

Transfixed as I was at our catch writhing upon the shore, I failed to grasp why Dad, apparently with the largest fish only, produced from his gear an ominously glinting fishing knife. In a flash of silver, the now unfamiliar phantom whom I called Daddy beheaded the innocent prize, our poor fish who'd done nothing more than try to eat a pretty fly scooting across a country stream. My heart leapt in dismay as scarlet blood oozed onto dry rock. I didn't know until Dad read the draft of this essay that my father's swiftness with the knife was a deliberate act of mercy. It bothered him terribly when others let their food die slowly by suffocating in a creel.

The dichotomy that I perceived in my father was the free spirit of a fisherman — juxtaposed with the war-torn soul of a teenager who had seen bodies all around him exploding. We had no idea. As children we felt secure. Our Dad took us on road trips and sang songs with us. He never talked about war. But once we'd matured into adulthood, our father's stories about World War II started emerging. In public talks, Dad began mentioning his nightmares. We heard the sorrowful stories of battlefield and Buchenwald. For many years now, Dad has had a pressing need to repeat his experiences for all who will listen. I've marveled at how my father was able to protect us as young children from the intrusive thoughts of the war that were with him all the time. Intrusive thinking is a classic sign of PTSD. In observing my father during my adulthood, I became inspired to specialize in the field of posttraumatic stress disorder. I know that Dad's repetition has nothing to do with "senility". On the contrary, the need for repetition is the price he pays for having a mind that is responding normally to the abnormality of war. Exposed to horrors as he was, and then coming home to a jubilant America, my father — like so many other returning veterans of any war — was not afforded the opportunity to process his experiences. It's encouraging to see that both the military and the mental health community are now making efforts to improve services for returning vets.

My father's story is both representative of the experiences of soldiers during World War II, and extraordinary in the number of such dramatic moments experienced by one person. So we, as his family, are very proud to see his book come to fruition; it's a project-in-process that he's had in mind for a long time. Not only is this publication a significant moment in my 86-year-old father's life, but it's an important statement for the current millennium.

During one of our sunset fishing trips, when in a contemplative mood, I sat at a distance from the shore while Dad fished. Noticing we were placed within a cliff-enclosed body of water, I understood the small circling winged creatures overhead to be bats rather than birds. Unafraid, I watched with interest. While my father swished his fishing rod back and forth in the standard swirling figure-eight motion used before casting, the bats seemed to make a formation and performed a complexly choreographed, smoothly graceful dance around the expanding reel and flexible rod. It fascinated me.

"Why don't the bats get hit by the fishing rod?" I asked. "Your line moves so fast, and the bats fly so close, but how can they know to fly between something so unpredictable?"

"It's because of their built-in radar," explained Dad. And he proceeded to explain to me, not for the first time, how bats don't have vision, but instinctively navigate by way of sophisticated internal sonar-like sensitivity. "Even when near quick and thin objects like rods and reels, bats have an uncanny ability to never run into anything."

And whack! Dad's rod was struck instantly; by a bat, of course, as if reacting to the words "never" and "anything". Dad and I froze in disbelief. Impossibility! And in that split-second of bat striking rod, like a baseball cracking with finality against its wooden player's bat, or the Zen master's boards clapping without warning to demand attention, my mind awoke to the fact that my father didn't know everything. Oh, he still knew a lot, sure; but not everything.

We laughed heartily. The bats had made a good joke on us. Yet the laughter was subtly different now. I glanced at Dad's shell-shocked face for a moment. It was as though the demons which had been haunting him since the war were suddenly reflected in his face by that unusual bat strike. Just like the fishing rod reverberating when striking the small, flying mammal, so too had my sensitive father been struck. Previously perfect, he'd instantaneously become fallible. He couldn't hide from me anymore. I could see his vulnerability. I was growing up.

My father lives in Georgia now, alongside a quiet lake, its autumn leaves becoming brilliant like my childhood sunrises. Dad has strung pulleys between the trees, creating a matrix of bird feeders designed for observation from his living room window above the water. And he feeds the ducks, dozens of ducks twice each day, from buckets of chicken scratch stored beneath the house. Cupful in hand, Dad stands on the shore and calls out in an assured nasal voice, "Quack, quack, quack, quack." Within moments, ducks come flying from each direction, landing in harmonious swooping splashes. It's rather remarkable. He's informed me that when he first moved there, before many other neighbors had built homes along the lakeside, Dad took out his treasured saxophone, the one he'd played in his army band during World War II, and proceeded to practice for pleasure on a summer evening; and to his great surprise, a flock of ducks flew over, like dancers at a wartime send-off party, to listen and swim together.

As for myself, I don't recall another fishing trip after that run-in with the flying bat, although it's likely there were at least a few more. Dad says he's never before or since heard of a bat running into anything, fast-moving or not. I don't for a moment doubt him on this. The day of the bat was the time to gently step down from my father's shoulders. I'm still stepping, of course, still stepping.

Nanci Rose-Ritter
October 26, 2011

Dedications

<u>My children Marc, Joe, Nanci, Mimi, Marty, and Wendy</u>, for listening to my "war stories" over the years. I know that sometimes my keeping The Pledge must have come at your expense. Most importantly, thank you for being, and having been, yourselves. Your mother would have been very proud of you. I know I am.

<u>Franny</u>, for being the girl whose letters and passion largely explain how I ever made it home, and for being the woman who became the mother of my children.

<u>My sisters Lois and Dorothy</u>, for conspiring to host me as successive college kids at U. Mich. Our conspiracy let me travel 400 miles to hear the incredible big band talent at Uncle Ike's theater. Mom and Dad never knew I stayed up all night during those eight years of visits, let alone starting at age 10. Oh, yes: and thanks for the three-part harmonies.

<u>Mom</u>, for looking after me when I was little, for your sense of humor, and for being ever active in community welfare.

<u>Dad</u>, for taking me fishing, looking out for my safety, and for being a volunteer leader of the USO, long before I was ever in uniform.

Acknowledgments

Wendy, for your encouragement, and for being the original scribe for the early stages of this book.

Marty, for inspiring us all through your incredible perseverance, and sense of humor.

Mimi, for sharing an interest in World War II, through the preservation and awareness of the art work of Nadia Werbitzky, whose family was confined to labor camps.

Joe, for your extraordinary ability to revere nature through your talents for photography and film developing.

Marc, for your community-consciousness, and for representing the underserved in your law practice.

Nanci, for your work with the American Red Cross, and as a mental health professional.

Sam and Dorrie, Sam for his help in obtaining image rights permissions and testing the eBook version on multiple platforms, and Sam and Dorrie together for their many brainstorming sessions on improving the safety and security of local children involved in after school programs.

Jessy Wheeler, reference librarian at the Boston Public Library (and her manager Gail Fithian), for your scholarship in clarifying the events surrounding the Buchenwald SOS, and for your enterprise in correcting the Wikipedia entry.

Jessalyn and Julianne, for your careful read and your suggestions.

Cathy, for instantly knowing what to entitle this book.

Credits and References

Cover Image Credits:

Snowy Hill image:
http://www.public-domain-image.com/nature-landscape/sunshine/slides/sunshine-on-snowy-tree-hill.html

Barbed Wire image:
http://creativecommons.org/licenses/by-sa/3.0/

Seedling Cutaway image by Mark Thiessen:
http://fineartamerica.com/featured/cross-section-of-soybean-seedling-mark-thiessen.html (Artwork: #18532)

Sunset From the Hill Image:
http://www.public-domain-image.com/nature-landscapes-public-domain-images-pictures/sunset-public-domain-images-pictures/sunset-from-the-hill.jpg.html

Image References

Image 1: Benny Goodman and his Orchestra at the New Yorker Hotel 1943
http://www.youtube.com/watch?v=r00AULUOZFo

Image 2: 87th Division Shoulder Sleeve Insignia
http://en.wikipedia.org/wiki/File:US_87th_Infantry_Division.svg

Image 3: Foxhole Illustration "Prone"
http://www.hardscrabblefarm.com/ww2/foxholes.htm

Image 4: Foxhole Illustration "Standing"
http://www.hardscrabblefarm.com/ww2/foxholes.htm

Image 5: SCR-300-A Radio Set
http://cyberreviews.skwc.com/bdmckay/wwii_scr300_fm04.jpg

Image 6: Photo from my Sister's Wedding

Image 7: The *RMS Queen Elizabeth*
http://www.ocean-liners.com/gallery/pages/qe.asp

Image 8: The Queen Elizabeth First Class Ballroom
http://www.thecunarders.co.uk/QE%20Gallery6.htm

Image 9: The Queen Elizabeth First Class Dining Room
http://www.thecunarders.co.uk/QE%20Gallery6.htm

Image 10: Landing Craft Tank
http://en.wikipedia.org/wiki/File:LCT202.jpg

Image 11: 40 and 8's
http://history.nd.gov/fgt/history7.html

Image 12: Barracks Bag
http://olive-drab.com/od_soldiers_gear_barracks_bag.php

Image 13: Spitfire Mark VII
http://en.wikipedia.org/wiki/File:Spitfire_VII_Langley_USA.jpg

Image 14: Crossing the Siegfried Line
http://en.wikipedia.org/wiki/File:Americans_cross_Siegfried_Line.jpg

Image 15: WWII Leggings and Shoes
http://www.usmilitariaforum.com/forums/index.php?showtopic=85513&mode=threaded&pid=628152

Image 16: WWII Combat Boots
http://qmfashion.files.wordpress.com/2011/03/boots_combat_ww2_03.jpg

Image 17: M-1 Rifle and M-1 Carbine
http://en.wikipedia.org/wiki/File:Garandcar.jpg

Image 18: US 761st Tank Battalion Insignia
http://en.wikipedia.org/wiki/File:US_761st_Tank_Battalion_insignia.png

Image 19: M4 Sherman Tanks
http://en.wikipedia.org/wiki/File:M4-Sherman_tank-European_theatre.jpg

Image 20: US 101st Airborne Division Patch
http://commons.wikimedia.org/wiki/File:US_101st_Airborne_Division_patch.svg

Image 21: King Tiger Tank
http://www.militaryfactory.com/imageviewer/ar/pic-detail.asp?armor_id=247&sCurrentPic=panzer-6b-pzkpfw-vib-tiger-ii_2.jpg&sCurrentDescriptor=Front right view of a King Tiger tank; note overlapping road wheels

Image 22: The Saar River
http://www.afhra.af.mil/shared/media/photodb/photos/080307-f-3927O-022.jpg

Image 23: Messerschmitt Bf 109
http://en.wikipedia.org/wiki/File:Me109_G-6_D-FMBB_1.jpg

Image 24: Rendering of Cut and Fill Railroad Bed Construction
http://2flowerspublishing.com

Image 25: Entrenching Tool
http://www.deactivated-guns.co.uk/militaria/wwii-usa-entrenching-tool/prod_128.html

Image 26: 3D Rendering of Foxhole Locations
http://2flowerspublishing.com

Image 27: Our position December 24, 1944
http://hallmouat.wikispaces.com/file/view/battle-of-the-bulge-map.jpg/141377479/battle-of-the-bulge-map.jpg

Image 28: Luxembourg
http://en.wikipedia.org/wiki/File:Luxembourg-CIA_WFB_Map.png

Image 29: Field Hospital Somewhere in Normandy June / July 1944
http://users.skynet.be/jeeper/page134.html

Image 30: The Purple Heart
http://en.wikipedia.org/wiki/File:Purpleheart.jpg

Image 31: Advertising Poster for Follies Bergere
http://vintageprintable.com/wordpress/vintage-printable-entertainment-recreation-2/art-poster-advertisement-entertainment-folies-bergere-4/

Image 32: WWI M1943 Field Pack
http://www.usmilitariaforum.com/forums/index.php?showtopic=2121

Image 33: Aerial View of Buchenwald 1945
http://www.chgs.umn.edu/museum/exhibitions/absence/artists/agalles/

Image 34: The Gates of Buchenwald:
http://history1900s.about.com/library/holocaust/blbuchenwald27.htm

Image 35: Inside Buchenwald: Ardean R. Miller, US Army Signal Corps
http://www.scrapbookpages.com/buchenwald/exhibits.html

Image 36: Artist Rendering of Shed Exterior
http://2FlowersPublishing.com

Image 37: Artist Rendering of Shackle Anchors
http://2FlowersPublishing.com

Image 38: Artist Rendering of Shed Interior
http://2FlowersPublishing.com

Image 39: Buchenwald Aerial Map Overlay
http://2FlowersPublishing.com

Image 40: Prisoner Badge Poster
http://upload.wikimedia.org/wikipedia/commons/6/68/German_concentration_camp_chart_of_prisoner_markings.jpg

Image 41: Prisoner Barracks at Bucheneald
http://www.scrapbookpages.com/Buchenwald/jedemdasseine.html

Image 42: The Ovens of Buchenwald
http://www.pbase.com/johnglascock/image/51738669

Image 43: The Bear's Den at Buchenwald
http://www.buchenwald.de/english/index.php?p=165

Image 44: Teeth from the Prisoners of Buchenwald
http://upload.wikimedia.org/wikipedia/commons/0/06/Buchenwald_Teeth_74565.jpg

Image 45: Lampshades of Human Skin
http://www.scrapbookpages.com/Dachauscrapbook/DachauTrials/ilseKoch.html

Image 46: The Small Camp at Buchenwald
http://www.scrapbookpages.com/Buchenwald/jedemdasseine.html

Image 47: Location of Maastrticht

Image 48: Switchboard Operator August 1943
http://ww2db.com/image.php?image_id=4780

Image 49: Maastricht City Hall 2008
http://en.wikipedia.org/wiki/File:Maastricht_2008_City_Hall.jpg

Image 50: Radar Scope and Operator
http://www.centennialofflight.gov/essay/Evolution_of_Technology/radar/Tech39G5.htm

Image 51: V-2 Rocket On Meillerwagen
http://en.wikipedia.org/wiki/File:V-2_Rocket_On_Meillerwagen.jpg

Image 52: Dornberger-Axer-von Braun
http://en.wikipedia.org/wiki/File:Dornberger-Axter-von_Braun.jpg

Image 53: Messerschmitt Me 262 Schwable the World's First Jet Plane
http://en.wikipedia.org/wiki/File:Messerschmitt_Me_262_Schwable.jpg

Image 54: "Ready for action somewhere along the East coast of the U.S., the crew of a heavy .50-caliber antiaircraft machine gun are ready to fire as their searchlight tracks a target flying overhead." ACME News photo dated January 6, 1943
http://www.skylighters.org/howalightworks/light1.jpg

Image 55: The Saxophone
http://en.wikipedia.org/wiki/File:DC3_Silh.jpg

Image 56: Douglas DC3
http://en.wikipedia.org/wiki/File:DC3_Silh.jpg

Image 57: Dick Arnold in his Eisenhower Jacket 1946
http://2flowerspublishing.com

Image 58: The Mona Lisa
http://en.wikipedia.org/wiki/File:Mona_Lisa,_by_Leonardo_da_Vinci,_from_C2RMF_retouched.jpg

Image 59: Cog Railway in Schneeberg
http://en.wikipedia.org/wiki/File:Cog_railway_Schneeberg.jpeg

Image 60: The Bombing of Nagasaki
http://commons.wikimedia.org/wiki/File:Nagasakibomb.jpg

Image 61: View of das Keh Kehlsteinhaus from north side
http://www.scrapbookpages.com/EaglesNest/exterior.html

Image 62: Entrance to tunnel which leads to the elevator up to the Eagle's Nest
http://www.scrapbookpages.com/EaglesNest/tunnel.html

Image 63: At the end of this tunnel is an elevator to the Eagle's Nest
http://www.scrapbookpages.com/EaglesNest/tunnel.html

Image 64: Waiting room outside the elevator
http://www.scrapbookpages.com/EaglesNest/elevator.html

Image 65: Liberty Ship at Sea
http://commons.wikimedia.org/wiki/File:Liberty_ship_at_sea.jpg

Image 66: Victory in Japan Day celebration in Times Square August 14, 1945
http://en.wikipedia.org/wiki/File:V-J_Day_Times_Square_NYWTS.jpg

Image 67: CEO Executive Forum Publication 1988 with Guy Hill

Bibliographic References:

Source material used by the Boston Public Library reference librarian, along with their comments:

Against All Hope: Resistance in the Nazi Concentration Camps, 1938-1945 by Hermann Langbein, with English translation by Harry Zohn

- *Against All Hope* uses primary source materials such as court testimony, personal narratives, and other official documents of the era.

The Buchenwald Report, translated and edit by David A. Hackett.

- *The Buchenwald Report* is comprised largely of Buchenwald prisoner interviews in the days immediately following the camp's liberation. The interviews were conducted by German speaking intelligence officers of the U.S. Army. Damazyn is not mentioned by name in the report. It seems as though not all prisoners knew about the transmissions. Those that did know about the transmissions seemed to not be aware of who exactly was responsible for them, beyond them being Polish.

About the Author

Richard Arnold held his first position of Editor-in-Chief at the age of 17, when he published a monthly magazine for The Manlius Military Academy called *The Windmill*. His next periodical, *The Countersign*, was a weekly magazine that he founded at Fort Jackson, SC in April of 1944 for the 346th Regiment of the 87th Golden Acorn Division. Later that same year, Dick published *The Elizabethan*, a daily newspaper created for the 15,000 men aboard the *Queen Elizabeth* as they crossed the Atlantic from New York to Scotland. In 1980, he published his first book *How to Solve Everyday Problems...With GOD's Help*, and has now kept a lifelong pledge with the completion of his greatest work to date, *Dig & Dig Deep*.

Currently, Richard puts his unique storytelling abilities to good use speaking to children and parents alike about the importance of freedom, and is often asked to speak in venues at VA associations, churches, synagogues, and schools all over the eastern United States.

www.ingramcontent.com/pod-product-compliance
Lightning Source LLC
Chambersburg PA
CBHW080554090426
42735CB00016B/3235